If we lose the Earth,
we lose our souls

———————

Bruno Latour

If we lose the Earth, we lose our souls

Translated by
Catherine Porter
and Sam Ferguson

polity

Originally published in French as *Qui perd la terre, perd son âme.*
Copyright © Éditions Balland, 2022

This English edition © Polity Press, 2024

English translation of the chapter "Ecological Mutation and Christian
Cosmology" © Sam Ferguson, 2024. Sam Ferguson asserts his moral right
to be identified as translator of this chapter. All other text was translated by
Catherine Porter unless otherwise indicated.

Polity Press
65 Bridge Street
Cambridge CB2 1UR, UK

Polity Press
111 River Street
Hoboken, NJ 07030, USA

ISBN-13: 978-1-5095-6045-5 (hardback)
ISBN-13: 978-1-5095-6046-2 (paperback)

A catalogue record for this book is available from the British Library.

Library of Congress Control Number: 2023939928

Typeset in 11/14 Sabon by Cheshire Typesetting Ltd, Cuddington, Cheshire
Printed and bound in Great Britain by CPI Group (UK) Ltd, Croydon

The publisher has used its best endeavors to ensure that the URLs for
external websites referred to in this book are correct and active at the time
of going to press. However, the publisher has no responsibility for the
websites and can make no guarantee that a site will remain live or that the
content is or will remain appropriate. Every effort has been made to trace
all copyright holders, but if any have been overlooked the publisher will be
pleased to include any necessary credits in any subsequent reprint or edition.

For further information on Polity, visit our website:
politybooks.com

Contents

Foreword

Once God has spoken,
twice have I heard this.

Psalm 62, 11

In the pages that follow, Bruno Latour addresses four challenges to Christians and theologians concerning the fate of the earth and of humanity. Known worldwide as a philosopher, sociologist, and anthropologist, Latour has spared no efforts to try to convince Christians to undertake a dual operation that is not self-evident. First, and this is the negative version of the challenge, he asks them to *pay attention to the earth*, at a time when it is being neglected. This implies that they should overcome their lack of interest in "earthly things," and that modern theology overall should be open to taking more interest in cosmology. Second, this time with a positive emphasis, he asks Christians to renew their apostolic teaching and their understanding of their faith in the context of the new image of the world that has emerged from earth system science. For, along with

vii

others, Latour has registered the seismographic *shock* of a representation of the world that describes not only the interdependence of the myriad beings that inhabit the earth but also the composition, by those beings, of a zone that living beings can inhabit: a slender, fragile membrane on the surface of the planet. Such an image of the world cannot fail to have a considerable impact on the sciences, on politics, and on "religion," just as, earlier, the cosmology of Copernicus and Galileo upset the old order. Given that renewal is an essential characteristic of Christian teaching, Latour sees in the ecological "crisis," and in the cosmological mutation that it entails, a "providential" opportunity to convey anew, to the largest possible audience, the evangelical "variation" in such a way that it can be understood in its originality and not confused with the old cosmology.

There are many reasons for assembling a work such as this one. First of all, it makes texts scattered among journals or collective works newly available, and to a larger audience. Second, by arranging them in an order that moves from the latest to the earliest, the book will enable readers to grasp the way the author's call proceeds not from a grounding theoretical adventure but rather from his attention to current history, to what might be called "signs of the times," signs whose meaning theologians ought to help decipher. And, ultimately, the publication of the work is meant to convey that call one more time, summed up in proverbial form in the title of Chapter 4: "If You Lose the Earth, What Good Will It Do You to Have Saved Your Soul?" For one has to acknowledge that, since 2008, when the first of these appeals was made, and despite the events that have marked contemporary environmental thinking, even despite the "divine surprise" of the encyclical *Laudato Si'* in 2015, theologians in the French-speaking world have not paid serious attention to Latour's plea that they face up to the cosmological mutation – unlike other thinkers throughout the world who have been making efforts to respond.[1] Theology and preaching carry on, here in France, as though nothing has changed, while among the faithful there are ever-increasing numbers who perceive the groans of the earth and who await help in discerning what the Spirit is saying to the Churches about these signs. The confrontation between theology and a cosmological revolution is certainly not without its challenges, as is apparent from the difficulties faced by French theologians such as Teilhard de Chardin or Édouard Le Roy when they tried to integrate Darwin's discoveries into their thinking. But Christian salvation and witness are now at stake. How many times can preachers associate summertime with rest and meditation on the "beauties of nature" when forests are on fire outside the sanctuary! And salvation is indeed what is ultimately at stake in the devastations of the earth. This small book makes that claim anew, humbly but firmly.

By standing back a little to consider the theological effort Bruno Latour is imploring his readers to make, it is not impossible to see it as a continuation of the work of the theologians who have had to "stitch back together" what modernity had taken apart through a series of abstractions. As we know, the moderns have a truncated picture of human beings, and a certain number of Christian thinkers have never stopped trying to "mend" that picture in order to restore its fullness. In the wake of Maurice Blondel's research, relayed by

Father de Lubac and other theologians, it was at first a matter of relaunching an effort to reweave anthropology together with theology, relocating the expectation of divine Revelation in the desire, consubstantial with the humanity of human beings, to see God. But that first "mending" no longer suffices to allow us to face the drama of the times with dignity. A second "mending" is required, one that solidly attaches anthropology to cosmology and avoids imagining that we can really be humans before we are terrestrial beings, or, worse, without having to be terrestrial at all. On the contrary, this second step affirms the extent to which the dignity of a human life presupposes that it is lived in a fully accepted terrestrial condition.

It is not unreasonable, either, to think that the role of these two "mendings," these two renewals,[2] is to verify and support each other mutually. The call to live the life of daughters or sons of God must not cut human beings off from the other creatures with which their Creator has connected them; quite the opposite: it should impel them into greater solidarity, for charity leads not to evasion but to incarnation. On the other hand, the fact that humanity is in community with myriad other creatures, however dense and normalized that community may be, does not suffice to assuage the human desire that finds its origin, its meaning, and its end in communion with Life and Charity. In publishing this little book, we hope that it will find and encourage readers who can help reconnect zones that have been kept apart: theology, anthropology, and cosmology.

August 25, 2022

Foreword

Postscript: Bruno Latour had reread and corrected the first proofs of this book a few days before he went into the hospital on September 29, 2022. His death on Sunday, October 9, 2022, prevented him from seeing it in print.

Frédéric Louzeau

I

The Great Clamor

Conversation with Antonio Spadaro, SJ

The philosopher, sociologist, and anthropologist Bruno Latour is an emeritus professor at Sciences Po Paris.[1] Translated into some thirty languages, Latour is unquestionably the contemporary French-language author with the widest readership in the world; his work on the climate crisis has made him a global presence on ecological matters, "the thinker who is inspiring the planet," as the weekly magazine *L'Obs* declared on its cover a few months ago.[2] We met at his home near the Odéon, at the heart of the Latin Quarter. A conversation imbued with wisdom and with the hope that is spread through frequent encounters with the big questions. A way of crystallizing more than fifty years of research, teaching, publication, and active commitment to the service of knowledge. A vision shared in the twilight of life.

On several occasions, in articles or talks, you have welcomed the prophetic character of *Laudato Si'*.[3] In what respect has this text by Pope Francis been relevant to your life as a researcher?

If we lose the Earth, we lose our souls

For me *Laudato Si'* was an impressive text from the outset. As it happened, it came out the same year as my book *Facing Gaia*[4] – too late for me to take it into account. For my part, I was trying to grasp what I call a cosmological mutation – but which is also a mutation in the relations among materiality, spirituality, politics, and so on, all those things that the changing perceptions of the world and nature subject to a questioning that promotes the terrestrial. I was astonished, in reading *Laudato Si'*, to discover the extent to which the prophetic and eschatological dimension of the new situation was magnificently expanded, quite explicitly, in this text by Pope Francis. He was making historical statements that were not unrelated to the COP 21 held the same year.[5]

This prophetic and eschatological opening onto questions in which I had more or less given up hope of interesting Catholics unsettled me deeply. It opened up the prospect of pursuing very important questions of theology and transmission, a whole series of topics that I had thought closed. Up to that point, the understanding of Nature that had prevailed during the three previous centuries had closed off themes of Christian spirituality that the new ecological situation was reopening. I found this fascinating. The Pope's text interested my ecologist friends, researchers in the fields known as the natural sciences, in a way that clearly allowed for a new dialogue that had been impossible, probably since the seventeenth century.

What is it in that text that connects with the emergence of the new cosmological situation?

Technically, the fundamental point lies in a new way of understanding living beings. By linking the cry of the earth and the cry of the poor, the Pope is on the one hand making a connection between ecology and injustice, and on the other hand acknowledging the fact that the earth is manifesting itself, that it can act and suffer. "[A] true ecological approach *always* becomes a social approach; it must integrate questions of justice in debates on the environment, so as to hear *both the cry of the earth and the cry of the poor*" (*Laudato Si'*, §49).

The Pope manages to reinsert a cosmological dimension into subjects that up to now, from a Christian standpoint – whether seen from inside or outside the Catholic Church – were treated as matters of morality. I have always been struck by the complete absence of the cosmos in modern theology, an absence that is paradoxically typical of secular society. Everyone had in some way lost the cosmological dimension. Abruptly, with the ecological crisis, the cosmos is coming back in with extraordinary intensity, among Christians as well as everyone else.

At the same time, in a second completely extraordinary revolution, so-called social questions about destitution, poverty, and so on are being newly articulated by the Pope in connection with this reappropriation of cosmological questions. In "official metaphysics," this conjunction is unprecedented. The poor who are crying out in lamentation are not supposed to have any relationship with the clamor of the earth.

So here was a shock and a transformational audacity that told me, to put it in my own terms, that we are both trying to change cosmologies, conceptions of the world, and that the two universes are going to be able to come into resonance at last.

> You argue in favor of a "Parliament of Things." I make the connection with the cry of the poor that is also the cry of the earth. They speak on behalf of the world. "This is why the earth herself, subjugated and ravaged, is among the most abandoned and maltreated of our poor; she 'groans in travail.'"   (Rom. 8:22) (LS §2)

This recosmologizing offers something of new interest to the sciences; it gets rid of the splinter in the foot that the Church has been dragging along for three centuries, that is, its inability to figure out exactly what position to take with regard to the natural sciences. This is what strikes me as the most innovative move on the side of the earth sciences. The impact of these new disciplines changes a lot of things; they open up a whole series of possibilities. They allow us to speak of the fact that the sciences no longer stem from "the view from nowhere"; they no longer define hegemonically a material framework onto which spiritual, aesthetic, moral, or other dimensions would be grafted as needed. Abruptly, the very notion of materiality has changed, and not without resonances. The Pope has mysteriously transported himself into this other cosmology that allows us to see that the cry of the poor and that of the earth are conjoined.

Many Catholics don't understand this. How can the earth cry out?

Yes, for many people this is just a nice metaphor; it is not constitutive, not ontological. But, from the standpoint of what I call the second scientific revolution, this actually makes a lot of sense, because the beings that make up the earth all have their own power to act; after all, by their involuntary efforts they have created the minuscule surface of the planet earth where all living things reside. And this action, spread over billions of years, as we are now suddenly discovering, has led to brutal reactions to our own human actions, and in a very short period of time. The long history of the earth and the short history of human societies are entering into resonance and into conflict. The reaction on the part of the earth is tipping us into a cosmological framework that had been closed off since the seventeenth century, despite all the revolutions in the history of the sciences.

So, this text is a real bombshell. Not that it is engaging in metaphysics, but it is positioning itself into a new situation, in which the interdependence of the beings that have little by little constituted our provisionally inhabitable world is a given. This is prophetic.

> *Which allows Francis to recall that the earth is a mother.* "Praise be to you, my Lord, *through our Sister, Mother Earth, who sustains and governs us ... This sister now cries out to us because of the harm we* have *inflicted on her ...*" (LS §§1–2)

Without being "New Age," however; without being metaphorical flights of fancy. I very much like Paul Veyne's observation that we are always talking about revolutions, evolution, and so on but, like people turning over in their sleep, we fail to notice that the situation is changing. We are suddenly elsewhere. You read *Laudato Si'*, you are elsewhere. And, from that point on, we are struggling to grasp, to metabolize, to understand, in order to recover that gesture. Unfortunately, there still aren't enough people who make the connection with the revolution in the earth sciences. People continue to live in the classic material world, because they're still living with the old way science was conceived, before the sciences became situated in the world in a different fashion. And people are finding it extremely hard to understand the revolution in the earth sciences. It's very discouraging; the message just doesn't sink in. I've made all kinds of efforts, nothing works . . .

And why doesn't it sink in?

I wish I understood. When you explain that living beings are the ones who have built the conditions in which they find themselves, that actually changes a lot of things. The earth, and what my colleagues and I call the "critical zone,"[6] was not especially favorable to the evolution of life; it has been made favorable by living beings themselves, beings that provided themselves with the needed conditions. The earth is not alive in the "New Age" sense, or in the simplistic sense of a single organism, but it is built, produced, invented, and woven together by living beings. It isn't a mere framework within which the living move around. When I look at the sky overhead, its atmosphere, its composition, the distribution of gasses, all that is the result of the action of living beings.

The phenomenon of changing cosmologies opens up the possibility of understanding differently some of the things the Pope is saying. The New Climatic Regime and the shock that the earth sciences are imposing on the understanding of the world opens a space in which the realities on high are significant for our terrestrial condition. In the seventeenth century, the Church allowed itself to be invaded by a science that is itself unearthly, offering a view from Sirius: this view imposes a conception of materiality that is immensely interesting for the understanding of our universe, but it lacks the hegemonic design needed for understanding what is happening on earth. The materialism of previous centuries, as we are becoming painfully aware, is in fact hardly material at all, or at least hardly terrestrial.

We don't live there . . .

We don't live there, there's no way to live there, even if it has immensely interesting effects on knowledge. It is important to go back to a conception that corresponds to the experience of living on earth. We are living beings, and mortals among living beings, and mortals that have constituted the very limited and confined little circle within which history has unfolded over four and a half billion years.

If Laudato Si' *is not being well received in certain Christian spaces, it's because we are still in a state of reaction in the face of a materialist and mechanical cosmology. The earth is only a background screen, finally. The Pope is asking us to convert to a new way of seeing in order to understand that the earth is like a mother and a sister, that we are in interaction. Have your colleagues also understood the text this way?*

We have had to read it, to exchange ideas, and it resonates differently thanks to the other contribution of *Laudato Si'*: the connection with the poor. If you make the connection between the classic social questions of inequality and the cosmological question in the sense we have just defined, that is, confinement in a positive sense – we don't live where we think we're living – then there is no way out. When people used to speak of cosmology, social questions were unrelated; they could be viewed as secondary. But if you make the connection with the new cosmological situation, you're in a space that is entirely defined and maintained by living beings. And so – this is the major theme of the Anthropocene – industrialized humans occupy an extraordinary place in this history. All of a sudden the question of charitable acts and the fundamental question of the poor take on completely new meanings, because they are no longer a residual problem. They constitute the problem we are going to have to live with. We won't be able to get away from it. It translates into heaps of topics such as degrowth, pollution, living conditions, and so on. But we're basically in a new situation. This time we're squarely ensconced in the social question.

In the run-up to the twentieth century, we were situated in time. We could always say: things are going to work out, the social question is very important, it will rise to the surface in the end. Now, we've moved into space, and a reduced space at that: it's fragile and active, it reacts to our actions at top speed. This recodes, in a sense, in a much more powerful way, the question of poverty, destitution, and inequalities of all sorts.

What is more, the whole world is finding itself tipped into a new cosmological situation and confronted with precarity. And this is terribly frightening. People are sensitive when you say to them: Are you aware that you are no longer in the world you were in before? This is very well described in one of the chapters of *Laudato Si'*. People who are already living in terrifying situations from the ecological standpoint, in addition to being poor, are subjected to ecological destitution. This is true in a certain sense even for the wealthy: the world is devastated for everyone – but the rich have the means to flee and hide, like Cain. The feeling of exile nevertheless runs quite deep. In the workshops I organize, it's very striking, people are all sensitive to the fact that there's been a turning point, we live here, but this is no longer where we should be living. The feeling is always translated by the question: What world are we going to leave our children?

The problem is that we've taken a very long time to become modern – roughly three centuries. It's normal for people to be traumatized when they're suddenly required to become "demodernized." In the seventeenth century, modernization meant nothing to anyone. We had to wait practically to the post-Second-World-War period for this phenomenon to take on hegemonic proportions in production. The phenomenon is really quite recent. For example, French farmers who have been modernized only since the 1950s are being asked to demodernize abruptly, as they're told that they are damaging the planet. It's a terrible trauma.

How is this cosmological overturning, this revolution, in fact good news for spreading the Gospel? Does this perspective re-open something for preaching?

In the Catholic universe, there is always confusion between the faith and its cosmological projection. When the cosmological projection is acknowledged by everyone, one can hear the intense versions of conversion, the act of faith, the act of charity. When the projections are out of phase, it becomes much harder, because one never knows what to believe in. *Laudato Si'* has arrived at a moment when the gap between the exigencies of faith and the cosmological framework is probably at a maximum.

Now, in an astonishing way, whereas the Church has been raising the question of modernity for about a hundred and twenty years, the project of modernization itself is collapsing! This doesn't solve any problems, because everything has to be reinvented, but it opens up an extraordinary opportunity to say that we have changed worlds, that everyone has changed worlds! We find ourselves in a situation in which the obsolescence of cosmological frameworks is common knowledge for everyone, inside the Church as well as outside. This situation has opened up the possibility of inventing new ways to inspire acts of faith, conversion, or preaching, other ways of talking about history, which is what the Pope is doing by taking up a whole tradition of the Gospel but putting it in different terms. The possibility is now open because, before, Christians were always paralyzed. Do we modernize, or not? Now we are encountering a situation in which uncertainty about cosmology is shared by everyone, and in which the project of modernization is in question everywhere. This doesn't provide a solution, but a space is opening up.

There is one point on which this space opens to a whole host of fascinating things: the definition of living beings. Before, living things were captured by biology, understood as a certain version of reductionism. Living beings, now, are those with which we find ourselves in the earth system and in the critical zone. They're no longer the same: they're agents that, by superimposing themselves on one another, have constituted their own conditions of existence and those in which we are forever immersed. Here we have an opening onto a large number of topics that I've been tempted to call matters of dogma; in any case, they're fascinating moral matters. The new situation makes it possible to understand differently a number of terms such as life, death, superimposition, cooperation, and so on, instead of simply asking "how am I going to manage to add a spiritual dimension to a material life that for its part has been left entirely on the side of a very impoverished version of the sciences?," which is the silliest and most paralyzing question there is.

Our problems as living beings are inserted into other problems of living beings; they're in some sense connected to the history of living beings. This brings up many issues, moral ones – of course Salvation – but also, more radically, issues that touch on the great story of Salvation. That story unfolds in a world that was initially mythical, then pseudo-scientific, with the scientific view of the world, and now we have to ask how we can re-tell the story of Salvation in a situation of terrestrial confinement. There are, fortunately, possibilities in incarnation; it's up to the theologians to find them . . .

This is something like what Pope Francis is doing. He's reincarnating theology and preaching . . .

He's placed himself in another world. But the theological elaboration of this matter is not his job. It's a colossal task, but very interesting. I think it ought to fascinate theologians.[7]

Lots of theologians are lost, because they were out-of-this-world.

Yes, they were off base, so moral questions necessarily prevailed. And, if we tell them now that perhaps they need to do a bit of earth science, which is being attempted at the Collège des Bernardins in Paris,[8] they're still going to be a bit lost, but they're going to get their bearings again very quickly and relearn how to move about in the world. They'll be much less lost than in the previous world.

Relearning how to move about in the world we are in: is this the goal of the workshops you have set up to sensitize people to the ecological question?

It's a matter of helping people to understand *where* they are, in a completely concrete sense. The temptation is to sound off in the abstract about the environment or political morality without touching the ground, whereas the New Climatic Regime and climate science push us to be attentive to the entanglements of the beings that constitute our soil, our habitat. These are shared exercises in the description of the conditions for life. What allows you to subsist? What are your means of subsistence? In what respect are these means of subsistence threatened? What are you prepared to do? Why? What are you doing to resist? These are very simple questions of sensitization and orientation, but approaching them collectively, without trying to find out immediately whether to set up wind farms or not, whether to separate one's trash or not, has truly therapeutic effects. We rediscover powers to act when we work together, without political discussions, to produce painful, difficult descriptions. These aren't workshops in which participants express their own opinions, but in which they describe, together, their own conditions of existence. Sharing this collective description of our terrain of life is the first step in a political articulation: being able to express common interests.

We've organized these workshops in a large number of situations: towns, parishes, cities, rural settings . . . At first, the participants claim that they subsist owing to completely abstract things, but by the third or fourth iteration these things become more concrete. They may involve a woman farmer whose water is polluted by the existence of a car-wash facility next door. Or someone who has an illness of unknown origin and who is beginning a lengthy quest to find out whether it is food-related or not. And so on. Every time, we observe a therapeutic effect, a conversion effect that makes it possible to take a step ahead.

If you ask people to meet to discuss vaguely green subjects, they talk about things that are utterly groundless because they don't know where they are. This leads absolutely nowhere. The situation is a new one, and people really don't know what to defend as their opinions, even if a multitude of convictions proliferate on social networks. The reconstruction of citizens who have common interests, and who are capable of expressing them in front of authorities who themselves listen to what is being said, requires a series of investigational arrangements that we are trying to build thanks to these workshops.

There's also a whole dimension of work on affects?

Yes, the passions associated with contemporary politics are very old ones, very sad, very narrow, not adapted to the ecological question, where one has to be interested in a lot of somewhat odd things, landscapes, ecosystems . . . So we're also working a lot with artistic methods for restoring basic expressive capabilities that have completely disappeared. The current isolation of individuals is such that they cannot even be citizens. A citizen is someone who sees other citizens and rubs up against them. We are trying to restore capacities for listening and capacities for moving about in space. These are absolutely elementary things, but they are essential. The goal isn't to expound on the dramatic aspect of the situation – I don't know what is going to become of my two-year-old grandson – but to reincarnate our existences. The participants need to be able to say: I have powers to act that I would like to make available.

Real spiritual exercises?

The *"Où atterrir"*[9] workshops or the workshops at the Collège des Bernardins are exercises, spiritual or ecological exercises in extricating ourselves from modernism. They are eschatological arrangements because they require participants to decide. Once again, space prepares one better than time for liberation.[10] It's now that you're doing what? The problem is that all these exercises, which are exercises in reincarnation, are not always perceived as spiritual exercises. This is the difficulty. And it's the source of the frequent criticism: why is the Pope concerned with these issues that are not "religious" issues? We hear calls to worry about the number of children in catechism classes, but not about the disappearance of wetlands! The idea that the problem of wetlands and the problem of teaching children the catechism can be grasped in the same spiritual question, one that is gradually emerging as the very definition of what it means to be Christian – this perspective is not in play. And yet these are the stakes of the incarnation!

What lesson have you drawn from the world-wide lockdown?

At the end of the lockdown, I published a book to alert people to the fact that, once we emerge from the health-based confinement, we'll enter into a planetary confinement.[11] We're in a different place. We're no longer in an infinite space, but rather lodged within the critical zone, in a situation where it turns out that humans are now a powerful geological force. Don't imagine that, once the medical lockdown is over, you'll be free from confinement from then on. You are locked down forever! This is somewhat anxiety-producing at first, but it's a way of saying: you live here, living beings have always lived here, living beings will always live here. There's no way out. Space becomes the apocalyptic horizon, and not simply time.[12] Decision-making happens now, precisely because there is no other space into which you can imagine projecting yourself later, as if all the acts of charity that you haven't performed in the present you'll be able to perform in the future. No, the time is now, as the Gospel says: it's now. The idea was very simple, and, once again, there is a sort of resonance, with possibilities that are opened up by the renewal of the earth sciences: they are reopening and defining a space time, a cosmology, within which all the questions of Christian preaching are raised in a new way.

The subject of confinement is a bit negative, but what is interesting is the terrestrial, a term that I am trying to make a common one: we are terrestrial beings, mortal living beings, and this is the hand we have to play. The earth doesn't interest the Moderns, whether they are believers or indifferent. This is also one of the reasons why some people have trouble with *Laudato Si'*. Why is the Pope interested in these questions of ecosystems and the like? For one thing, it's not a religious topic; and then it isn't very interesting, or in any case it's less so than escaping to Mars. In fact, to become interested, one must already have changed. This is why exercises are necessary, because all at once people see things differently and tell themselves: Ah! This is where I'm situated. Questions of defending the environment, which seemed abstract and overwhelming, given the immensity of the problems, suddenly become concrete: this is the world I'm in.

It's curious that it takes so much effort to be materialists. We were supposed to have been materialists during the modern period! In fact, we were no such thing; we were dematerializing ourselves, abstracting ourselves, and conceptualizing an abstract world – one that has a lot of useful functions within scientific networks – but that is not the earth. With the new ecological situation, we are coming back down to earth.

And here the question for believers arises: what is the impact on the history of salvation? This is the very interesting underlying question: can there be, after the medieval periods, after the modern periods, a new period in which the Church can institute itself in entirely new civil relationships with the other modes of existence, and not try to install itself within a morality, a politics, a science. Here is a fine subject for theology. I don't know why, but I feel, more than others perhaps, how hard, even impossible it is to talk about these religious questions with people I'm close to or with my contemporaries. What can be done to make these words audible? At bottom, we no longer know whether what matters is belief in a cosmology or hearing words of conversion. To be sure, the discourse of conversion works on its own: like water, it spreads everywhere, into all the cracks. But still, preaching is supposed to be audible. Pope Francis has opened up a space with his text.

You've been doing research for more than fifty years. How do you understand all that you have lived through, if you look back over your trajectory?

I've simply discovered that there are several regimes of truth that the moderns have discovered and that they don't know what to do with (I've limited myself to about fifteen). My philosophical discovery lies in my having explored these different modes of truth for fifty years, systematically.[13] Don't go looking for hegemony in the type of truth you've inherited. This doesn't mean that the other types are false, but they're in another mode of existence and have to do with other beings. No development of religious truth can impinge on political truth, which can't discredit scientific truth, which for its part can't discredit moral truth. It's a discovery that suffices to justify a life of research, no? No one has ever grasped, in a non-hegemonic way, let's say, the plurality of modes of truth. This is what I have been doing over these fifty years. And the question becomes whether this plurality of modes of veridiction can finally be instituted.

We're in the twenty-first century, in a situation that is changing. We have acknowledged, learned, understood the extraordinary power of scientific truth, the extraordinary necessity of political truth, the formidable power of fiction, and now, with ecology, the formidable, essential, and substantial existence of the beings involved in reproduction. A possibility that was closed off before is now opening up, that of instituting religious truth as well, without asking of it more than it can give, but without taking away from it anything it has to offer.[14]

2
Ecological Mutation and Christian Cosmology

Presented at the International Congress of the European Society for Catholic Theology, Osnabrück, August 2021.[1]

Since I am unable to speak as a theologian at this conference, I am addressing you as someone who has tried to grasp what the ecological mutation is doing to philosophy; and also as someone who has always been inspired by Catholicism, and has been frustrated at being unable to transmit its message to my loved ones. So, in this lecture I shall try to link these two crises: that of ecology and that of transmission. I want to see if a different understanding of the mutation currently under way would make it possible to revisit the message from a different perspective. I will proceed in three stages: in the first part I will define the contrast between cosmological projection and preaching; in the second part I will list some points where, in my view, the change of cosmology provides a new opening for certain traditional questions of transmission and preaching; finally,

If we lose the Earth, we lose our souls

I would like to summarize the present situation, as I see it, by presenting a riddle that will, I hope, open up the discussion.

I

Any change in cosmology presents an opportunity for Christian preaching to renew both the form and the content of its message. We are now living through a rather radical change of cosmology, of which the painful experience of Covid–19 is the most powerful expression.

At the risk of overdramatizing, we could say that we have gone from a cosmology whose canonical model is Galileo's experiment of calculating the fall of heavy objects on an inclined plane, to a cosmology whose canonical model is that of a virus that keeps passing from mouth to mouth, spreading from one person to another, forcing all societies to change their behavior, and which is constantly mutating. The old mechanical models no longer occupy the center of our interests, and it is now instead living things (and above all, viruses and bacteria) – which are capable of transforming their own conditions of existence to the point of bringing into being, over billions of years, an inhabitable terrestrial world – that are becoming the focus of all our concerns and all our knowledge. The Galilean tradition of an earth moving through infinite space is now replaced with an earth that "is moved," in every sense of the word,[2] an earth that reacts to the actions of those particular living things called human beings, and that raises the existential question of whether or not these humans will be able to maintain the conditions of its habitability. It seems to me that such a change in world-views cannot fail to alter the framework, the direction, and the expression of Christian preaching.

The first thing that is revealed by the ecological crisis, which I call the New Climatic Regime,[3] is that there is perhaps no necessary, definitive, indissoluble link between Christian preaching and the *cosmological projections* through which it was often expressed in the past. By "cosmological projection" I mean the Grand Narrative of what the catechism called the "Holy History," which elaborated a magnificent account of the world, leading from Creation to the End Times. This account, which is depicted in paintings in count-less churches, still has the power to overwhelm both art lovers and believers through its magnitude and fullness. However, it is precisely this fullness, this complete-ness, this magnitude that prevents us from grasping the substantial rupture that has been introduced by the emergence of the new question of maintaining the world in a state that is habitable for humans and their fellow creatures. Cosmology (this time in the classical, theo-logical sense) covers everything, but that is precisely the problem: it *covers too much*, and it too quickly covers over the key problem of the era we have collectively entered. The Holy History can no longer play out in the same way if there is no longer a terrestrial world where it can take place. This is why we must slow it down for a moment and allow it to incorporate a new discontinuity into its Grand Narrative.

This discontinuity can be seen quite clearly when we realize that the Gospel message, by definition, is com-pletely *indifferent* to any cosmology. This is why I use the term "projection." The cosmological framework is an amplification, by means of a narrative or story, of a message whose radicality obeys completely different *rules of verification*. Indeed, it is the particular feature of the beings who convey this message in their preaching that they are *sensitive to the word*, and that their truth is found in their ability to convert those whom they address.[4] Where there is no conversion, there is no truth.

To use the central example so much liked by Ivan Illich, the Good Samaritan becomes the neighbor of the wounded man who has been left behind by the priests, and it is in this very act that lies the truth of the interaction; not in the matter of ethnicity or adherence to any worldview.[5] Becoming the neighbor of the wounded man, without hesitation and without worrying about his own urgent affairs, defines the situation and consequently breaks the spatio-temporal framework in which the other three protagonists, as well as the Samaritan, are situated. The question of final ends is played out here and now, and therefore also the question of salvation. In such a situation, the cosmological framework is not only irrelevant, but it is rather the very obstacle that the act of charity breaks. The continuity of preaching rests on just such acts of charity, which, through transmission from one person to another, are capable of establishing – to summarize all too briefly – a whole *people of saved neighbors*.

In relation to this continuity, cosmological projections serve as *altar of repose*, a kind of place holder, to summarize the situation *while awaiting* the resumption of acts of charity. It is such acts of charity that *verify* the quality of the act of faith, rather than the spatio-temporal framework by which it was summarized for a time. By definition, this framework belongs to the domain of common sense, whereas, also by definition, the act of faith breaks with this same common sense. This is precisely where the distinction between the two movements can be detected: whereas we adhere to the spatio-temporal framework, as an object of belief, the act of faith demands that we convert those we are addressing, that we become their neighbor. The two elements are not in continuity with each other. And above all, they do not age in the same way. Cosmological projection varies in space and time, whereas, by definition, the act of preaching modifies space and time, since it founds the moment of salvation, the attainment of final ends. It is in this sense *universal* (or at least universalizable), but only if it succeeds in converting those to whom it is addressed, whereas cosmological projections are, by definition, *relative* to a time and a people.

It is clearly this radical discontinuity between the act of faith and belief in a spatio-temporal framework that explains why each change of cosmology forces both preaching and theology to start over again. When the two are in phase, the problem does not arise: if the rich young man in the Gospel gave up following Jesus' call, it was not because of any problem in understanding the framework in which the Master was expressing himself – they shared the same framework – but rather because the imperative demand of the preaching asked of him something that he refused to follow, "for he had great possessions."

The situation is obviously very different when the two are no longer in phase. Each receiver of the preaching will then have to decide whether to adhere to a framework that is alien to them, or whether to allow themselves to be transformed by an injunction that transforms them into a neighbor, an injunction that breaks with the frameworks of the two protagonists. The Samaritan and the wounded man have nothing in common, except precisely that which makes them neighbors to each other in spite of the frameworks associated with their respective identities. When the distance between cosmological projections and the act of faith becomes infinite, preaching becomes impossible, time is wasted in unravelling what depends on one and what depends on the other, and the interlocutors find themselves separated indefinitely. They have then missed the opportunity to encounter the Gospel message because they have been asked to believe first in the framework in which it is currently collected and simplified – even though the message itself breaks with this framework! It is as if the Good Samaritan had first asked the wounded man to convert to his sect before binding up his wounds . . . In times of cosmological crisis, the situation becomes more and more tragic, the Gospel message literally becomes *inaudible* – at least when it is directed *ad extra*, toward those on the outside, the very people to whom the message is addressed.

I will take this gap as the starting point for the second part of this lecture, by asking whether the current crisis might offer an opportunity to reduce the gulf that separates the message from its current expression.

II

The most common cosmological projection today, or at least up until the prophetic rupture introduced by Pope Francis's *Laudato Si'*, is based on the rearrangements made during the modern period to accommodate the concept of Nature as being subject to laws. Indeed, it was largely a reaction to the influence of modern science that gave rise to: the opposition between transcendence and immanence; the emphasis on the destiny of souls rather than that of the world; the obsession with questions of morality in parallel with a growing lack of interest in the fate of the cosmos; the fear of ecology; the dread of paganism; the Church's retreat into a search for identity; and, above all, this strange idea that, faced with the Grand Narrative of Nature proposed by Science, it was necessary to promote an alternative Grand Narrative that presented a different, more "spiritual" and less "material" version of world history.

Although these rearrangements may have seemed necessary from the seventeenth to the twentieth century to resist the deanimation of the world imposed by scientism, they may no longer be necessary today, now that the very concepts of "matter" and "materialism" have been thrown into crisis by this new cosmological transformation. From the moment when the key question becomes that of the earth's habitability, we realize that the materialism of the previous period was hardly "materialist" at all, since it had forgotten, obliterated, denied the role, the scope, the importance, the fragility, the intermingling of living things, which are alone capable of constituting, over the course of millennia, the envelope necessary for prolonging the terrestrial story. The earth sciences no longer have much to do with "Science" (with a capital "S") as it was still imagined in the twentieth century, and against which theology had tried to draw up an alternative Grand Narrative.[6] Fighting against "materialism" seems a very outdated task when, on the contrary, we must learn to rematerialize, in a thousand different ways, our belonging to the Earth.[7] This immense rupture in conceptions of the world offers theology the opportunity to rethink, once again, as it has always managed to do in times of crisis, how to accompany the renewal of preaching, now that this preaching is liberated from cosmological projections that no longer correspond to the demands of the time.

And it is perhaps with time that we can begin a first inventory of these transformations. In an important but little-known book, Vítor Westhelle underlines the astonishing tropism of modern theology for the *temporal* dimension, which has made eschatology into a theme that is almost exclusively linked to the Grand Narrative of the Holy History.[8] As if eschatology were not a *spatial* as well as a temporal theme.

For the Good Samaritan, the wounded Jew is just as eschatological, is just as much a mark of final ends, limits, boundaries (this is the meaning of the word *eschaton*) as the Grand Narratives of the End of the World, with their special effects, angels, trumpets, and resurrections, which perhaps preoccupied the priests who passed by the wounded man in their hurry to go and fulfil their obligations in the Temple. But what the New Climatic Regime decisively brings to the fore is precisely the question of *limits*, and the terrible demand that these limits should define the *final* ends. This era is coming to the realization that it has no time to wait. And, consequently, that any narrative that minimizes the spatial demand of eschatology in favor of a projection in time betrays, in fact, the very demand of salvation. What is the use of saving your soul if you end up losing the terrestrial world? The cry repeated every day by earth scientists in an increasingly strident manner, "it's now or never" (and repeated once again this month in the latest IPCC report), cannot fail to resonate in an infinitely tragic way for every Christian soul. And especially in light of the indifference of so many Catholics who are convinced that the disappearance of the terrestrial world is essentially "irrelevant" to the question of Salvation, since they are convinced, in any case, that they will always be able to turn "to Heaven."

Nothing shows more starkly the absolute disconnect between the cosmological projection of the Holy History and the demands of the act of faith than this inversion of the very *direction* of the relationship between Earth and Heaven. In the old tradition, Heaven obviously did not mean only an ascent on High, but, above all, a break with all kinds of belonging, all cosmological projections. *Caelum* in the sense of Heaven was not to be confused with *caelum* in the sense of sky. The fact remains that, from the time of the modern compromise, in order to resist the so-called "materialism," Heaven came to designate an escape from the world. It seemed that we would turn our attention on High once and for all. A whole imaginary, a whole art, tens of thousands of sermons, hymns, and prayers, a huge apparatus of metaphors, conditioned reflexes, mental images, a whole "ascensionism" toward the High, whereas a concern for the Earth – the real "Holy Land" – supposedly led souls down below: now or never, there or nowhere.

This astonishing inversion in the model of the end times goes against the grain of ordinary forms of faith and ritual, and it cannot fail to have consequences for theology and even dogmatics. This "new" earth, which was the object of such great hope, appears today in *all its newness*, but in a totally unforeseen form, that of a tiny envelope, infinitely old and fragile, woven by the intermingling of living things, and which we must learn to care for so that it does not disappear altogether. It is no longer the object of a distant eschatological expectation, but that of a present action that judges each of us just as sharply as the rich young man in the Gospel story, asking: "What have you done with the world?"

What paralyses this redirection down below is obviously the strange theme of the supposedly "stifling" nature of immanence[9] in relation to the necessary "elevation" toward transcendence. Yet the opposition immanence/transcendence is itself also an artefact of the cosmological projection invented in reaction to the concept of Nature. At the time, it was necessary to insist on a "supplement of soul," as a correction to the so-called "materialist" version of modern scientism, a conception that limited life to the narrow confines of biology.

Yet the living beings that we must learn to take care of today bear no resemblance to the living beings of the Darwinism of the past. Those beings belonged to Nature, they were supposed to adapt to an external environment, they obeyed laws that were superior to them, and, in particular, the supreme law of natural selection, which was a barely secularized form of Providence. The whole challenge for Christians therefore consisted in "escaping" the grip of these living beings in order to really exist *as humans*. But today's living beings have a completely different pedigree: they made themselves by gradually constituting, through their own intermingling, the conditions of habitability that are favorable to them.

It is these living things that have produced the environment, including the soil and atmosphere. To "escape" from their grip is therefore meaningless; you might as well not want to exist at all. They do not belong to Nature (a half-concept, the other half of which is, of course, Culture). They are the world they have given themselves and in which we humans are well and truly enveloped. As a result, "immanence" is no longer a direction whose opposite would be "transcendence." This world of living things is as "transcendent" as it could possibly be, in the very real sense that their interactions constantly "transcend" themselves. Every day we discover the power and fragility of their "transcendences," including in the tragic experience summarized by the now well-known term "the Anthropocene."

It is this very special transcendence that was so aptly described in Saint Francis of Assisi's famous *Laudes Creaturarum*, in which he celebrated not only "Sister Moon" and "Brother Wind," but also "our Mother Earth," and finally "our sister bodily Death." There is a strange familiarity between the New Climatic Regime and the incarnation. The ecological crisis is a *prolongation* in the very direction to which the incarnation already pointed. Salvation is movement toward abasement, kenosis. What is at issue are the limits of anthropocentrism, limits that are found both in the classical theme of man's dependence on his creator and in the current theme of man's dependence on the living beings that have gradually, over billions of years, constituted the provisionally habitable world into which man has inserted himself. Obviously, this overcoming of anthropocentrism was impossible as long as the ecological turn was associated with a "cult of nature." The contradiction with the Gospel message, as well as with the ordinary cosmological projection, was too manifest. But, in the end, ecology has little to do with Nature, that seventeenth-century invention produced in order to provide a framework for the cosmological transformation of the time. Today, ecology is no longer a matter of Nature at all, but of caring for the beings on which we depend and which depend on us, and whose destiny is not regulated in advance by any higher Law. The incarnation immerses us in a story of intermingling with the living beings whose salvation now depends in part on the acts of charity that we can perform without postponing them on the pretext of "another world": now or never, here or nowhere. If Christians fail to respond to this bifurcation, it means that they prefer to cling to the cosmological projection to which they are accustomed, and so to sacrifice the Gospel message which they have been called upon to take up.

It is not only the concept of Nature from the last three centuries that paralyses this descent, this abasement, this kenosis, but also the unhealthy fear of "paganism," as if by embracing a care for the Earth we would "fall back" to the level of idolaters. And yet, the concept of paganism is like that of Heaven: what had been a necessary contrast at the time when this new form of truthfulness was emerging (which therefore leads Jan Assmann to refer to Christianity as a "counterreligion")[10] has become in the modern era a kind of colonial fantasy, like the "barbarian" of ancient times. Paganism exists only in the eyes of the civilizers and modernizers. But those who are disparagingly labelled with this term *preceded* the counterreligions by many years in their concern for the cosmos. Whereas, just a few decades ago, indigenous peoples were considered to belong to the past of peoples who were unanimously marching toward progress, now those same indigenous peoples are *ahead of us* in the search for a way of caring for the world that we now share with them. There is an *antecedence* of religious traditions here that should be the subject of just as much work as was done, from the very beginning of Christianity, on the antecedence of the Chosen People. (This also explains the significance of Pope Francis's prophetic gesture of asking members of Amazonian peoples to plant a tree in the Vatican garden in October 2019.)

Despite its long history of iconoclasm, the Christian counterreligion has no reason to quarrel with cosmological religions that depend on other models of truthfulness and aim at quite different goals. The desire for the world to continue can no longer be considered to be an error or a moral failing. The "pagans" have therefore gone from being irreconcilable enemies to being our brothers in the shared task of maintaining the habitability of the terrestrial world.

These are the few points that I felt it was important to mention in order to point out the distance, which is now vast, between preaching and the cosmological projection that served as its provisional support. With regard to the eschatological dimension of time and space, the concept of Nature, the opposition between transcendence and immanence, the conception of living things, and the tense relationship between religions and counterreligions, we can measure the extent to which the New Climatic Regime is overturning the ordinary cosmological projection that remained roughly stable throughout the nineteenth and twentieth centuries. In many respects, the current mutation resembles, with respect to the dimensions that are affected, if not its actual content, the mutation that took place in the seventeenth century, when religious souls had to absorb the new cosmological conception linked to a certain Grand Narrative of Nature proposed by Science. This is not at all to say that the new earth system sciences finally offer the ideal framework for preaching to adopt, as if the message had to be adapted once again to scholarly truths, for the second time. It is simply that the shock that these earth sciences bring to our understanding of the world, and in particular to the concept of Nature, opens up an unexpected space where the classical questions of theology can breathe more easily, without being constantly forced to defend themselves against "materialism." The interest of the current Covid–19 pandemic lies in the possibility of playing the role of a troublesome gadfly, mosquito, or wasp on all these issues, in order to remind us constantly that we have, once again, changed the world and that it is high time that we took notice.

III

I have often wondered, in pursuing the anthropology of the Moderns, why this form of preaching that is the soul and spirit of Christianity has never finally found an institution that is truly its own. It is true that the fragility of its movement, this highly demanding dependence on the capacity to convert those to whom it is addressed, which is the only means of ensuring the truth of what is said, may prevent it from stabilizing itself in an institution tailored to it. Hence the temptation, always rejected and, at the same time, to which the Church has always had to give in, to rely on other, apparently more stable, forms of truth: political, moral, juridical, economic, artistic, mythical, scientific, each of which served as a placeholder, a relay, a storage place, before the resumption of preaching. This explains the importance taken on, over the years, by the various cosmological projections, accounts, and Grand Narratives that seemed to summarize the content of this paradoxical and radical message in a form that was more comprehensible and, above all, less demanding than preaching.

What is changing today is that we are coming out of the modern parenthesis. As we know, the clergy have long been concerned about whether or not Christianity should be "modernized" to "adapt it to the times." By an extraordinary stroke of luck, it is the whole of modernization that is collapsing before our eyes today! We are therefore justified in asking whether the time has come, by taking advantage of the shock of this new cosmological mutation, to institute preaching – to use a trivial image – "within its own home," and no longer surrounded by the trappings of the other modes of truthfulness. It would then no longer be a question of adaptation, compromise, or arrangement, but of inhabiting again.

As I am unable to draw theological lessons from these probably too disjointed remarks, I would like to offer you a riddle by reusing a well-known figure, that of the Garden of Eden. What would be changed in the Gospel message if we were to assume that the Christian God arrives in a Garden that has *already been there* for a long time, a luxuriant Garden that has developed, over billions of years, through the intermingling

33

of living beings capable of providing one another, without having willed it or actively pursued it, with the conditions of habitability that ensure, year after year, the continuation of their adventure? This Garden symbolizes the antecedence of living things and the key question of the conditions of habitability that they themselves have created. It is in this lush garden that a tree is planted, a tree *among others*, known as the tree of knowledge of Good and Evil. This knowledge *adds* to the other forms of truthfulness a crucial novelty, that of final ends, of salvation, and of the relation to a neighbor that breaks with all belonging. The neighbors who are saved by this new form of discernment form a people, among other peoples, mixed among them. The history of this people neither summarizes nor covers that of all the others. But it certainly *adds* to it. The question then becomes whether this people destroys the Garden from which it is excluded, like someone who saws off the branch on which they are sitting (we recognize here the old figure of the Fall and the Expulsion), or whether, on the contrary, this people is capable of engendering new variants, new species, new cultures, which enrich its diversity and ensure its continuity over time. A tree among many others, a variety of truth among others, certainly indispensable once it has been established, but without the privilege of definitively summarizing all the others. This would be a major event, but one that could not harbor any hegemonic ambition. The question I would like to ask you is therefore very simple: would such an implantation make the message *audible* again to those who no longer have any key to decipher the cosmological projections that are used to explain it today?

There you have it; I have tried to link the two concerns I summarized at the beginning: a strong impression of the ecological mutation currently under way, and my fear that I am unable to share the message with my fellow human beings.

3
On a Decisive Overturning of the Schema of the End Times

By way of a prologue: reorienting iconography

Alas, Neo Rauch has not authorized me to reproduce his painting "Der heilige Franziskus Bergoglio Märtyrer erhält die Hommage an Gaia" ("Saint Francis of Bergoglio, Martyr, Receiving Homage from Gaia") a work that would have been a magnificent introduction to my essay. In his inimitable style, Rauch went back to the old tradition of martyr paintings – in the left-hand corner we even find a dried palm frond, a direct allusion to the traditional theme and an unmistakable citation of a painting by Caravaggio. But Rauch, with his passion for enigmas and emblems, succeeded in entirely overturning the meaning. Whereas in paintings on the theme from the Christian tradition we see the sky open up at the top of the canvas, from which – with lots of clouds, bright flashes of light, and whirlwinds of angels or cherubins – we can see the reward of eternal salvation, there is nothing of the sort in this new version of martyrdom. The main character, seriously contorted by pain, seems to be headed *toward the bottom* of the canvas, and it is from a violent black form with violet and reddish overtones that he seems to hope for his salvation.

No doubt about it: this is indeed a portrait of the present Pope Jorge Mario Bergoglio! It was astonishingly daring of the painter to have canonized Pope Francis before his death, but Rauch offers us the reason in a part of the painting on the upper right, where we can discern a muddled crowd with "Santo Subito!" ("Sainthood Now!") on the placards. Rauch's iconography is unmistakably inspired by that of the "Petit Pauvre" (Jacques Copeau's rendering of St. Francis of Assisi), just as Copeau's iconography was inspired by that of Christ. At the center of the canvas we even find the luminous, insipid colors of Fra Angelico, without being able to tell whether they are mocking the tradition or paying it homage. In any case, Bergoglio is perfectly recognizable by his face, even if his clothing resembles a Franciscan homespun smock rather than a white cassock or pallium.

As always with Rauch's work, the interpretation is complicated by the proliferation of levels, anecdotes, and citations. What is certain is that this particular Francis is suffering greatly, and that his two hands point to the lower part of the painting without making it clear whether he wants to go there or to move away. It is all set up as though light and salvation – but how can we be sure whether light and salvation are in question here? – were coming from below, and as though the Saint is headed in that downward direction, unless he is being pushed by a crowd of people who seem to surround him and who might be supporters or opponents; it is hard to tell.

The enigma becomes somewhat clearer when we read the label and realize that the subject is a martyr. And yet Saint Francis, the one from Assisi, the model for Bergoglio, was not martyred at all, and if he ended his life in fasting and prayer, it was in his own bed and in his own good time. Why this strange idea of making Bergoglio a martyr fleeing downward, a direction that throughout all Christian iconography usually designates hell and all its darkness?

The answer can be found by inspecting the crowd behind the new Saint Francis. In one group, people are clinging to the saint's garments as if obliging him to come back and stand up, as if they were actually trying to put him in the usual position of the person who is waiting to receive the martyr's palm from above. The faces of the characters, some of whom are wearing miters and others caps, indicate a state of fury and indignation, as far as we can tell. But perhaps this is a projection imposed by the viewer on the painting in response to the many disputes Bergoglio has stirred up, as we know, within the Church. What confirms my diagnosis is that Rauch drew a sort of pallid phantom that unmistakably resembles the emeritus pope, Joseph Ratzinger. Rauch is playing with the image of the pope and the anti-pope, but without our being able to tell which is the good one and which the bad ... Here we find again the habitual style of a painter who takes pleasure in piling up ambiguities.

Still, the part of the crowd that seems to be headed unmistakably toward the lower right, an area some philosophers call "the terrestrial," sends a clearer message. Here we can make out excited young people straight out of a chromolithograph from the past illustrating the "children's crusade" – Rauch loves to borrow from the clichés of medieval fairy tales. These figures are all tugging on Francis's habit or clinging to it. They are helped by rows of "natives" in "Indian" costume, with feathers and tattoos, but also, as far as one can tell, by nuns in black and white bearing big red crosses; they seem to be praying loudly or pleading with the martyr Pope to head toward the shadowy mouth that is opening up like an abyss under their feet.

What makes the painting unreadable – and explains why, when we saw it in Rauch's studio, we couldn't decide on its message (and this is probably what accounts for the continuing embargo today) – is that Bergoglio's face is evenly divided between mystical enthusiasm and horror! As if Rauch had fused the ecstasy of Saint Theresa with the terror of one of the damned who sees the mouth of the devil in hell opening up in front of him. The work is indeed a last judgment, then, or in any case a judgment of Pope Francis, but without giving us any way to be sure of whether he is saved or condemned.

The enigma would be cleared up if one could reconcile the title with the dark red spot that presumably represents the point toward which the Pope is heading and that Rauch designates by the name "Gaia." Even if one approaches the still fresh canvas, it is impossible to make out any figure that might resemble the mythological one. Nothing in any case that would justify the title of a homage rendered by Gaia to Pope Francis. It is this magisterial uncertainty that explains the unspeakable suffering that emanates from the martyr's face and indeed from the entire painting. There is no doubt, in any case, that this is one of Rauch's masterpieces and the first, to my knowledge, to open up a new direction in Christian iconography. What a shame that it remains unknown to the public.

"Laudato Si'" does not deal with ecology

Here I would like simply to start from *Laudato Si'* and reflect on the originality of the anthropological – and also theological – proposition advanced in Pope Francis's encyclical. I would like to approach that text by showing that it introduces a decisive reversal in the schema of the end times, a reversal whose consequences seem to me to have been insufficiently developed (and whose impact on iconography might have been made visible in Rauch's work). In approaching the question of what the Anthropocene does to the theology of Creation, it goes without saying that I have no particular qualification for dealing with the two elements I propose to link, except that I have followed the literature on the Anthropocene fairly closely.

It would be tempting to situate the encyclical within an ecological movement, as if Pope Francis had "become aware," in a more insistent way than his predecessors, of the importance of the crisis facing living beings and had sought to add this crisis to the list of issues with which preaching ought to be concerned. Now, to say that he produced an ecological text would, to my mind, mean missing its flavor – and by that very token missing the opportunity to open theology to new terrains. If ecology cannot be the point in this matter, it is because the text concerns a change in the notion of world itself, and thus in the notion of nature. It is the concept of the *terrestrial* that turns out to be modified in a durable way, along with the framing functions of time and space. This is the proposition I mean to stress.

The originality of *Laudato Si'* lies in the invention of a figure that is in fact a new one, in which the "cry" or the "clamor" (translations differ) of the earth and of the poor are expressed. A true ecological approach always becomes a social approach; it must integrate questions of justice in debates on the environment, so as to hear both the cry of the earth and the cry of the poor (§49, p. 35).

This double cry or clamor forcefully signals that the *figure* in question has little resemblance to that of the "nature" that is at the heart of traditional ecological preoccupations, nor does it have much to do with equally traditional theology (I shall come back shortly to the notion of figure). As far as I know, the earth as envisaged in the old climatic regime does not have the capacity to cry out, and no one would have dared designate it by beginning with the lovely expression borrowed from St. Francis, "sister mother earth."

> "Praise be to you, my Lord, through our Sister, Mother Earth, who sustains and governs us, and who produces various fruit with coloured flowers and herbs." (§1, p. 3)

Which Francis then comments on as follows:

> This sister now cries out to us because of the harm we have inflicted on her by our irresponsible use and abuse of the goods with which God has endowed her ... This is why the earth herself, burdened and laid waste, is among the most abandoned and maltreated of our poor; she "groans in travail." (Rom. 8:22). (§2, p. 3)

If this new figure of an earth that groans under the action of humans is so original, it is because it is mixed indissolubly, in the encyclical, with the cry of the poor.

Now, two hundred years after the birth of what could be called the preoccupation with ecology, and despite all the efforts of militants and thinkers, the link between the destitution of the poor and the ecological catastrophe or mutation still remains very weak. The social question and the ecological question exist in a relation of branching or even contradiction, as if it were necessary to keep on choosing between economics and ecology: a choice well summed up in the slogan of recent political demonstrations in France on the disconnect between "the end of the world and the end of the month." In *Laudato Si'*, on the contrary, the indissoluble link between two new issues – the cry of the earth and that of the poor – is the very object of new apostolic attention.

So it is clear that we are not dealing in any respect with a text about which one could say: "Look, a pope is finally interested in the question of nature." No, we are dealing with a prophetic innovation in which a pope introduces a new figure that displaces the old theme of nature, the one that was previously shared by ecologism as well as by the enemies of ecologism. He brings this new object to the attention of Christians: the clamor of mother sister earth and of the poor. We need to reflect on this originality without rushing to make it traditional or inoffensive. The comparison between this encyclical and the texts with ecological content of Francis's predecessor, Benedict XVI, sheds light on the difference, moreover: the argumentative style of the latter clashes with the flow of prophetic images in the former.

The cry of the earth and of the poor

When we are contending with radical innovations in the forms of preaching, we cannot settle for a doctrinal commentary that would bring novelty into the tradition without renewing the tradition itself. That would be the case if we were to look at *Laudato Si'* as a text concerned with "nature," something that had to be respected or saved. This is why, before taking stock of its originality more precisely, it is essential to insist on the link between the cry of the earth and the cry of the poor.

That the earth is capable of crying out is at bottom what is expressed in a cooler but no less militant and no less engaged way by the controversial term Anthropocene.[1] As huge as the transformations imposed by humans during the Holocene (the last 12,000 years) were, they affected the human environment and not the earth system itself. The involvement of the earth system in human history – geohistory – defines in more scientific terms what the encyclical calls a "cry" or a "clamor," let us say a groaning that can be studied and calculated.

In a pioneering text, Michel Serres had already brought to light this "earth that is moved" (in French, *s'émeut*, "moved" in the emotional sense), in contrast to the expression attributed to Galileo: "and yet the earth moves" (in French, *se meut*, "is in motion," i.e., it changes its position in space).[2] There is enough here to unsettle the best-established certainties. One has to agree to acknowledge that all the efforts at preaching, all the rituals, all the ecclesiastic institutions, all the metaphors with cosmic content, were developed during the Holocene – they have never had to confront, literally and not just figuratively, an earth that is moved and that cries out. The term Anthropocene is a mnemotechnical device to help all those who run into indifference and denials, who mutter under their breath, safe from new inquisitions, "And yet it is moved . . ." So, the encyclical might be seen as the most flagrant example of what the Anthropocene does to theologies of Creation.

Now, the innovation of *Laudato Si'* is that it directly attacks the greatest limitation of the contested term Anthropocene, a too quickly conceived hybrid of anthropology and geology. Where the now somewhat tedious critics of the term (I prefer to speak of the New Climatic Regime, to stress its legal and institutional dimension)[3] get it right is that the humanoid agent, the *Anthropos* of the Anthropocene, remains an abstract being, a generic human, an empty universal. Everyone agrees that it would be completely unfair not to take into account the unequal distribution of responsibilities and impacts alike. Overall, the least responsible are the most affected. Consequently, by associating the cry of the poor with the cry of the earth, Pope Francis refrains from simply going along with the mode of the Anthropocene; he reorients the concept by connecting it with the long history of the Church taking the side of the poor. The innovation in *Laudato Si'* is that it seizes the major geohistorical innovation – which is indeed the earth system that groans and is moved – and links it to the apostolic concern that is as old as Christianity.

One can understand why the encyclical is so radical and that it defines a quite distinctive way of taking up the overworked theme of the "common good": it is not the same "common" – for the earth is getting itself involved – and it is not the same "good," nor, above all, is it *the same evil*. It is hardly surprising that every effort has been made to hasten to bury words that are so radically prophetic, as our account of Rauch's imaginary painting has endeavored to show.

Where are the realities from on high to be found, from now on?

It is time to explore the consequences of such a novelty for preaching. I stress preaching and not simply theology or philosophy. For, as it happens, one cannot speak legitimately about religious themes without judging them by the yardstick of preaching: their degree of truth or falsehood depends on their capacity to convert those to whom they are presented. For example, how are we to understand the Letter to the Colossians, read on the last Sunday of the Easter season: "So if you have been raised with Christ, seek the things that are above, where Christ is, seated at the right hand of God. Set your minds on things that are above, not on things that are on earth, for you have died, and your life is hidden with Christ in God" (3:1–4)?

I realize perfectly well that philosophy and theology can find a thousand ways to explain these dated expressions by putting them back in their context, just as exegesis will be able to explain the formula "seated at the right" as well as the trope of the "things that are above" – and these disciplinary glosses will all be correct. Yet it remains true that such interpretations amount to informed evasions in the face of one huge fact; the radical textual contrast is indeed this one, as today's ears hear it: "Set your minds on things that are above, *not on things that are on earth.*" In terms of the reception of the word, one cannot be clearer about the order and nature of preferences, about the direction of the gaze imposed by these metaphors, about the priority to be granted to one virtue or another – once again, for today's ears, which have become totally ignorant of the ways of preaching in the Christian tradition.

The question is thus how to reconcile this figure with that of exclusive attention to the earth and the poor, who are groaning together about the same injustices. "Set your minds on the realities of the earth, and no longer at all on those that are above." It would be much too simple to settle for inverting the spatial schema. "If you lose the earth, what good does it do you to save your soul?"[4]

And yet, if we have actually passed from an old to a New Climatic Regime, we cannot continue to pour the same metaphors into the same old wineskins; we cannot settle for tinkering with the meanings that have been given the terms "things from above" and "from below." A change of epoch or of era like this one implicates everything else. It cannot be denied that in *Laudato Si'* there is an inversion in the overall structure of every act of preaching, sensitive to the joint cry, partially unarticulated, of the earth and the poor, suffering in the same groaning. As in Rauch's painting, Pope Francis is pointing toward something new that is located, in the metaphoric order of things, unmistakably "below" and not "above." In any case, there is no doubt that the encyclical designates a new horizon. There is a complete change of direction, a change of vector in time as well as in space.

To size up the current situation, it is marked, in one way or another, by the impression that we are headed *downward* after a long period when we seemed to be moving away from any limit and, in sum, seemed to be flying in the sky. "To land" is becoming a verb that defines an epoch. It seems that we are terrestrializing ourselves in a new way; we are drawn toward a new attractor. The old idea of the earth conceived as a globe, like the old idea of matter, is no longer relevant to the earth that we now have to inhabit. Hence the importance, as I see it, of the sciences of the earth system, the crucially innovative rediscovery of Gaia, and the term Critical Zones, which does not define nature but rather the delicate skin of the terrestrial globe on which everything that has lived and will ever live is disposed.[5] It is by no means a question of contrasting cold, objective sciences to the subjective world, but rather of choosing among the sciences those that allow us to understand in new ways the astonishing difficulty of living in these critical zones that react so rapidly to our actions. The earth we are beginning to discover thanks to these sciences no longer bears any resemblance to that of the ponderous materialism the "spiritualists" loved to hate.

Schema and figure

As always, when we have to exercise some discernment in reflecting on innovation and the ecclesiastic tradition, we have to go back to the distinction between what could be called a *schema* and what I have been calling a *figure*. A schema, in itself, is mute; it says literally nothing without the figures that alone modulate it, express it, embody it, decline it in myriad ways according to the circumstances of the preaching. But by themselves these figures say nothing if they are not attached to the schema that they express provisionally and always more or less awkwardly since they lack the ability to translate it directly. We cannot trust any one of these figures to help us discern what new figure will comment rightly on the previous one unless we *return to the schema*:

47

this is the only means by which it is possible to judge the fidelity of the figure in and through the renovation of expression. Without going back to the schema, there is no way of telling the difference between mindless reiteration and repetition. This is, *par excellence*, the major lesson imparted by the twentieth-century French Catholic poet Charles Péguy.[6]

The great power of the text *Laudato Si'* is that it makes the schema newly perceptible behind the figures of tradition, because of the direct and explicit reintroduction of the theme of the apocalypse into all questions having to do with the ecological crisis (or, more precisely, the New Climatic Regime). I am not alluding here to the accusation, brought by disaffected parties and skeptics against the ecologists, that charges them with "giving in to apocalyptic thinking"; I am referring rather to the simple return of the question of the end times in all moral, social, and political issues, and also – here is the big surprise – in every scientific subject. Once again, this theme becomes contemporaneous with history, or rather with geohistory, in a still more powerful, more imminent, more exigent way than in the epoch of the threat of a nuclear holocaust (a threat that coincides exactly with what is called the short Anthropocene, which dates back to 1945, according to the stratigraphers, and which continues to hang over our heads as it did at the height of the Cold War).

The return of eschatology is a total surprise for people sensitive to ecology – whether they are militants or scientists – because they most often refuse to take any interest whatsoever in any story or consideration that strikes them as "religious." Even those who appreciated the fact that Pope Francis "finally showed some interest" in their subject were indignant about the passages in which he reutilized the tradition. The common sense of my ecologist friends, whether historians, philosophers, sociologists, or geochemists, holds that we have to advance on all these questions without going back through the "old Christian stuff." And among this old stuff nothing horrifies them more than eschatology.

Now, the superiority of the schema of the end times is that today it traverses the entire field, whether we are dealing with the beliefs or lack of beliefs on one side or the other. I know no practitioners of these matters who do not have their own eschatological view of the present situation. It is in this sense that the schema renews all the positions: finally, "the end of the world" once again becomes the name of the new question concerning the Common Good; more exactly, it seems that our common good is quite precisely the end of a world. Lacking a world: here is the new universality.[7] An objective, material, calculable, datable return of the question of the end in every sense of the word "end": I am also speaking of *finality* and of *definitive judgment* as well as of *goals* to pursue.

Although it is contradictory to seek to designate directly the schema expressed by the figures of tradition, it is precisely in a period of crisis that one can best perceive it for an instant behind the obsolescence of the figures. To summarize it in a sentence, one might say: "in the time that is passing, a time that does not pass is bursting in." And of course there is a corollary: we are dealing with an impossibility, since time keeps on passing. Consequently, it is necessary *always to begin again* to express the schema by multiplying the figures, conveying both its truth and the necessity of taking it up again on a new basis in order, literally, to follow, to accompany the time that is passing, to adapt to the logic of the time that is passing, by recalibrating, time after time, the same paradoxical and always necessarily misunderstood message.

This schema can be grasped, historically, only through contrast with the civic or cosmic religions that are attached to a totally different phenomenon: how to manage to endure, how to maintain oneself in existence, how to discipline, to master the time that is passing. The durability – today we would say the "sustainability" – of their societies, of their civilizations: this is the concern to which religions had always been attached. Until the appearance of these other religions – Jan Assmann explicitly calls them counterreligions, moreover[8] – that have been devoted to working on another schema, that of the accomplishment or the judgment of time – within and in spite of the time that is passing. Hence the relative lack of interest on the part of the new religions in civic and cosmic continuity, and their insistence on the figures of the end times or the end of time. In their eyes, it is a matter of ensuring not durability but rather rupture, and thus liberation from all questions of continuity: "The end times have come." Here we can spot one of the origins of the "things from above" whose role is to contrast with the "earthly things" St. Paul was talking about. What is in question is obviously not a relation between below and above in an actual spatial sense, but between what lasts definitively, definingly, and what passes; between what judges and what is judged.

The New Climatic Regime, while it allows us to re-use the schema, obviously overturns the figures that have allowed us to express it up to now. If there are secrets that from now on everyone is seeking somewhat desperately to learn, it is how to manage to last, to maintain, to obtain continuity, to sustain societies against the threat of an end time, one no longer hoped for but alas achieved for real by the very action of humans "liberated" beforehand from the cosmic and civic constraints of tradition. The old "realities from on high" have become "out-of-this-world" postures: indifference to the crisis, denial of the climatic situation, indolence, and escapism.

In a stupefying and completely unforeseen fashion, the end time has burst in, not as the realization of a promise finally fulfilled from above; not as the always-renewed expectation of a truth that cannot be accomplished without betraying itself; but as the realization, alas factual, objective, temporal, of a reality for which humans – certain humans more than others – are alone responsible. Not for a second do we have the right to forget that the end time is a reality for a very large number of species. It would be particularly disgraceful to want to replay the scene of Francis preaching to the birds while holding up to today's fowl the promises of the apocalyptic Revelation, given that so many of those species are in the process of disappearing for good, victims of that sixth extinction of which we have become the agent.

The distribution of values along the schema has been reversed, as we can see. It is probable that formerly, in St. Paul's time, for example, what we might call the "vertical" dimension of the end time was marked positively, and the "horizontal" dimension, to remain within the clichés of Sunday sermons, had a negative value. The hierarchy of attachments was such that one had to prefer to attach oneself to the realities on high rather than to those of the earth below. Today, though, the end time does not represent liberation from cosmic constraints, nor does it mean emancipation from all civic interdictions; on the contrary, it means flight out of this world and a stubborn refusal to hear the clamor of the earth and the poor, humans and nonhumans alike, deprived of all continuity, all protection, and any durable identity. A general crisis in engendering.

To put it bluntly, *it is transcendence that has become misleading*, not to say diabolical, and it is immanence – that immanence scorned by centuries of "spirituality" – that is becoming desirable in moral and civic terms. From now on, the horizontal dimension has precedence over the vertical. What clearly had not been foreseen when the figures of "above" and "below" were invented and then validated by tradition is that the end of time could result from the emancipatory action of humans themselves, an "apocalypse of civilization," as Eric Voegelin has called it,[9] and not at all from the return in glory of a Son of God. Here is what obviously changes everything; here is what explains why, in the picture I have dreamed of getting Rauch to paint, the finger of Pope Francis would not point to the sky but to the earth, the old and wholly new earth of the incarnation, which lies helplessly in the groanings of a continual and increasingly painful effort to give birth.

New figures of immanence and imminence

I should like to draw three lessons from this reversal in the values attributed to the figures of the schema of the end time – a schema that obviously remains the same, since we keep on scrutinizing its power and its contradictions through constantly renewed figures, without ever being able to approach it directly and without ever eliminating its contradictory character.

The first lesson entails revising the traditional positions concerning the much-vaunted paganism against which we would have to continue to fight in order to maintain the no less-vaunted "vertical dimension." If there has been a tragic error of target choice in the history of the counterreligions, it is to have seen in paganism a figure in competition with those counterreligions for truth (something that Assmann has seen with admirable clarity), whereas it was actually a question of a set of cult practices oriented toward entirely different values, values that, in the New Climatic Regime, suddenly take on great importance.

"Paganisms" – whose forms, virtues, weaknesses, even crimes, are countless – in fact aim at immanence, but not in the sense attributed to it by the claim to transcendence, By immanence, paganisms mean continuity, the prolongation, the survival of cosmic and civic forms of life warranted by the divinities, about which everyone has always known, without any subterfuge (contrary to the accusation of idolatry), that they are obviously – and fortunately – made by human hands.[10] On this point, rather than serving to enlighten, the hatred of idols has instead induced blindness.

If we are starting to look at these paganisms with some envy – after they have been pitilessly eradicated almost everywhere, and continue to be attacked by missionaries – it is because we are desperately seeking that sort of immanence once again. Whatever one may say about the immense virtues learned from the counterreligions, whether in their missionary and Christian forms or in their lay, modern, secularized forms, the least one can say is that they have not put forward the key question of their survival, their durability, their temporal continuity! They have plunged into the climate crisis without a moment of reflection. They are joyously disinterested with respect to their terrestrial condition, and, worst of all, they believe that they have found their greatest virtue in this lack of interest . . .

The point is obviously not to return to the pagan cults, which have been destroyed or in any case totally eviscerated, but to stop fighting them, to understand their modalities so as to begin to learn from them how to survive by deactivating some of the poisons of the counterreligions.[11] The fear of paganism has slowed down and sometimes even paralyzed attention to the terrestrial. To the question "Will Mother Earth require human sacrifices?" we must not hesitate to reply that millions of men and women have been and continue to be sacrificed to this forgetting of immanence in the name of the atrocious transcendence of "out-of-this world." These are the sacrifices that must be brought to an end first of all.

The second lesson, related to the first, entails restoring the question of *rituals* to its key position in any new approach to preaching. In fact, and I am fully aware of this, the schema is not expressed particularly well in the language of argumentation – to speak of "the end of time in the time that is passing" is to say nothing – but it is expressed in a privileged way in rituals (and all the better, it goes without saying, in a good life and through the practices of charity without which we would be nothing but "clashing cymbals"). To speak of the Common Good without speaking of the rituals that build commons is to speak into the void. Where are the rituals, the ceremonies, the hymns that have made use of *Laudato Si'* to make evangelical preaching comprehensible, not to those on the inside, *ad intra*, but to those, *ad extra*, for whom it has become totally foreign – I am referring of course to the vast majority of our fellow citizens, since complete non-comprehension of Christian preaching has become the default position today.[12]

Now here is where one bumps into the set of metaphors, hymns, gestures, invocations, prayers that continue to lean on a classical contrast between the realities on high and that of the earth, without taking into account their recent reversal. How can one not be startled upon verifying, during the most recent celebration of Good Friday, that the prayer said to be "universal," covered its subjects one after another, except for the most universal of all, that of the mother sister earth groaning under our blows? If there is a ritual to be invented, that is the one. A problem of composition, different every time, and one that moreover has to come to grips with the sciences of this earth reconfigured by the Anthropocene. If one wanted to simplify the goal to be pursued in the reinvention of rituals, one could say that it is a matter of combining on a new basis the *figures of immanence* and *those of imminence*, the ancestral holiness of the world and the new urgency of not making it disappear. Especially because these rituals have to make it possible, finally, to designate the enemies, explicitly but not vengefully, in the countless current conflicts, and those to come, over the occupation of lands and climate wars.[13]

The third and last lesson entails learning how to seize the opportunity for a renewal of the very conditions for preaching, an opportunity offered by the New Climatic Regime and the reversal proposed by *Laudato Si'*. The schema of the end time has long exerted a powerful impetus of liberation and emancipation, in contrast with the effects of civic and cosmic religions. We have to recognize that, starting in the modern era, because of the unfortunate competition with the sciences, the schema seems to have been lost in the clouds. In any case, it has remained powerless to struggle against the false transcendence of the "out-of-this-world" and of the more and more pronounced and more and more criminal indifference to existence on earth. Set off against the temptation of the "out-of-this-world," the appeal to the "realities on high" has begun to ring false, or has even come to evoke absolution for the crimes committed. Let us recall that climate skepticism, or what I have called climate quietism, is still very widespread among Christians and more or less required in America for those who claim to be preaching the Gospel.

This has been the case prior to the current situation of reversal of values between transcendence and immanence. Now, abruptly, preaching inspired by the schema of the end of time has recovered its full force, provided that it seizes *immanence* as incarnation and *imminence* as struggle against the out-of-this-world. It is no longer a matter of waiting or preaching the Apocalypse, but of *preventing the end of time,* in the totally practical, mundane, objective, material form of the disappearance of the earth, the soil under the feet of humans and the other beings with whom they share it. A return to the great question of the *katekon*, of the capacity to slow down, to suspend, to delay the end time, which is no longer before us as something hoped for, but is rather, in an unforeseen sense, *behind us,* as a leap into the abyss. Is it not, moreover, this power to slow down that the children who go on strike every Friday invite us to exercise in order to avert the catastrophe that will deprive them of a future? To prevent the end of time, to plunge into the realities here below, to immerse ourselves instead of emancipating ourselves, to learn to depend: such is the rediscovered movement and energy of apostolic preaching. The schema is always the same; how could it be different? But its figures are all new.

Back to the beginning

It is through this return of energy, directed now toward the new figures of incarnation, that we can take the measure of the prophetic character of *Laudato Si'*. It would be a mistake to shove the New Climatic Regime back into the usual apparatus of doctrines and rituals, while thinking that it is a matter of the same old "nature," scarcely transformed, just a little more colorful, a little more insistent, a little more tragic. No, it seems to me that this new figure of the world offers the opportunity to preach, finally, *ad extra* and no longer *ad intra*, by making the old schema of the *end times* once again comprehensible to the multitudes. The originality of geohistory lies in its disclosure of a situation that is not unrelated to the beginnings of Christianity.[14]

4

If You Lose the Earth, What Good Will It Do You to Have Saved Your Soul?

And the Church does not defend herself merely by her doctors, her saints, her martyrs, by glorious Ignatius, by the sword of her faithful children;

She appeals to the universe! Attacked by robbers in a corner the Catholic Church defends herself with the universe! Paul Claudel, *The Satin Slipper*

A few months ago, I was attending mass at St. Thomas Church – the parish that serves the strange University of Chicago campus, which is an enclave in a vast Black ghetto – when I was surprised, at the moment of the Universal Prayer, or Prayer of the Faithful, to hear the celebrant ask us to include in our intentions the "depollution of Lake Michigan"! It was the first time I heard someone pray in a church for the success of an ecological action . . . Was I entitled to think that Lake Michigan, which had been sterilized for two centuries by all sorts of pollutants of human origin, had just taken its place among the poor, the ill, those gone astray, in the long list of those usually included in the intentions of the

58

Universal Prayer, at this point in the Catholic mass, in the heart of the congregation? And, if Lake Michigan, emptied of all organic life, was also to take its place in the list of those who suffered, was I to conclude that the list of sins that we are capable of committing was also to be extended that far? Having contributed in the past to the pollution of Lake Michigan, having slowed its depollution in the present or even having remained insensitive to the importance of the stakes, had these become, for these parishioners of St. Thomas Church, new sins that they had learned to confess, for which they sought to be pardoned?

No, I did not wryly take the unusual intention in that prayer as a weird New Age gesture that would have lured the hipsters at the University into a chic version of sin. I felt, on the contrary, the appeal of a question all the more urgent in that it reminded me of a scornful reflection ventured by Ronald Reagan's Secretary of the Interior, James Watt, who was responsible after all for protecting the environment. To justify his decision to open up national parks to massive exploitation by loggers and to the development of huge above-ground coal mines, he had responded that it was quite useless to protect them since, he claimed, Christ was going to return within a few generations. Why bother, indeed, since it's all going to disappear anyway; we might as well allow our friends in Big Business to make some quick profits. In 1981 this was, I recognize, a very unsophisticated version of the theme of the Apocalypse, and not a very religious version at that – a vulgar American remake of the French monarchic maxim "*après moi le déluge*": after me, the floods.

It is possible, however, that James Watt was simply saying out loud, in a trivial, mercantile form, what many churches keep on advocating in forms that are seemingly very elevated, very spiritual: everything that is transitory, carnal, material, fleeting, temporary, this whole world of deceitful appearances, matters less than what lasts; and it is to what lasts, what is eternal, what does not deceive, that we must entrust our hearts' treasure. Is this not what preachers still tell us on Sunday about that injunction of the Gospel, whose meaning I have allowed myself, not without some trepidation, to invert and use as the title of this talk: "What will it profit them to gain the whole world and forfeit life" (Mark 8:36)? Isn't spiritual development in its entirety turned toward what lasts at the expense of what is transitory? Isn't it toward the Heavens that we turn our gaze whenever someone speaks to us of the life of the spirit? Who among us, if we were to ask them to paint the ecstasy of sainthood, would have the bizarre idea of having the saint look not toward the sky but toward the ground?

But what if we were mistaken about how to interpret this injunction? What if we have read the Holy Gospel as badly as we have read the second book, that of Nature? What if the "lasting development" of our souls did not mean abandoning the Earth to the benefit of the Heavens but meant rather another way of dealing with the transitory, the fleeting, the fragile?

To introduce these big questions I have neither the necessary erudition nor – most crucially – the necessary piety. (The only exegesis I practice is that of scientific texts and scholarly Scripture, which is less familiar, alas, than Holy Scripture.) Instead, it is through a meditation on a series of paradoxes in which I find myself immersed that I claim to speak; let's say that I represent those who turn to the theologians and the exegetes to ask this simple question: "How are you going to deal with the ecological questions?" Or perhaps, with more intensity: "Why have you, the guardians of the Incarnation, ceased to be interested in the Earth, even though, we are told, we are soon going to lose it?"[1] Or, to press even harder: "What good will it do me to save my soul, if I or my children or my grandchildren have lost the Earth?"

You will perhaps object that ecology rarely figures in programs of theology. I'll reply that the issue does arise, since you often speak of eschatology and morality. Am I not somewhat justified in thinking that the moral sense will change direction depending on whether one seeks to turn toward the Heavens or toward the earth? Am I wrong to think that all traditional morality is suspended, or at the very least renewed, by the question of the end times? Is this not the very object of a great deal of current and pressing research?[2]

I don't think I'm exaggerating when I say that what has been the particular object of research for many theologians slipped out of their grasp long ago: it has become the common concern of millions of people who are completely ignorant of the etymology of the words "gospel" or "apocalypse,"[3] and who have long since left the rites of churches behind. The discourse on the end times has been generalized, so to speak, over the last few decades, to the public at large. There is hardly anyone today who doesn't worry about the announced disappearance of the world as we have known it. And this annunciation of the End Times is not Good News, a gospel, but very bad news, a counter-gospel. The euphoric version of the Apocalypse, which James Watt was naively expecting to deliver him from the obligation to preserve the national parks of the United States, finds itself inverted in a dysphoric version by people known as the "prophets of doom," who are mockingly accused of presenting an "apocalyptic vision" of the evolution of the planet. A new report comes along every week or so whose highly technical content is literally eschatological, since it announces, in detail and with statistics, the end times, or at least the end of our way of life. Whereas formerly, in the "good" version, the woes of the times were to be succeeded at last by the coming of the Kingdom, in the "bad" version the Apocalypse is going to put an end to happiness, to the carefree old ways of life.

What the threat of a "nuclear holocaust" – another biblical term transposed into common usage after the end of the Second World War – did not manage to make us feel, we are feeling now, owing to the proliferation of ecological crises: "The end time is near." To be sure, this new end time no longer benefits from all the Hollywood special effects that are supposed to make us shiver, and those that imbued St. John's Apocalypse with its aesthetic force. From this standpoint, the nuclear threat (under which we are still living, moreover, in total indifference) looked more like the demonic scenography of the sacred texts than like today's multiform ecological threats. In nuclear extermination there was something instantaneous, something so radical that one couldn't even tremble before it any more than before one's own death; people were terrorized, of course, but they forgot about it right away. "I think about it, and then I forget." It's something else again to begin to lack water, air, space, wheat, credit – not all at once but through a slow, low-temperature apocalypse, as it were, and one that, more seriously, no longer depends on the decisions of a dozen leaders in whose rational character, despite the irrationalism that permeates the overall situation, one could still believe; it is a question of the present action of billions of humans in whose rational character it is impossible to trust. The nuclear threat relates to the ecological threat as sudden death relates to a long illness: the abrupt disappearance in the first case terrifies us much less than slow degeneration. Another major difference between the two "Apocalypses": the nuclear holocaust remained suspended above our heads and in the future, while the ecological end of time is visible in everyone's garden, supermarket cart, television set, and bank account. We're in it. The end time has become close again. "With all their bombs, they've ended up messing up the climate": it was easy to make fun of the old loudmouths making such claims. But we're there. The loudmouths were right . . . and so, even, was Philippus the prophet, clothed in his sheet, and the gong that so terrorized Tintin in *The Shooting Star*.

Ecological eschatology, the discourse on the end of the old ways of life (and from now on the term "the old ways" designates the modern, or rather modernist, way of life, the one that claimed to be putting an end to all the archaic anxieties about the end of the world and replacing them with progress, with glorious tomorrows) – this discourse (for I'm really talking about a discourse) in fact differs from all the others in that it has as its source *the very people who are also its victims*. I don't believe I'm mistaken in affirming that the traditional apocalyptic themes feature the more or less sudden arrival of a cataclysm from the outside that falls on the poor humans who may, of course be responsible for it by their malicious intentions and their sins, but who are never the direct agents of their own destruction. The fire that falls upon Sodom and Gomorrah comes from on high, after all, and destroys cities. Here too one can say that the nuclear holocaust closely resembles that habitual staging of the drama, since the "nuclear fire" unleashed by authorities protected in underground bunkers fell upon the poor populace like divine fire. (And it is moreover in that quasi-divine power that political power cloaks itself with the right to life and death over all of humanity, the power that had the right to push the famous button.) The ecological end time has a distinctive feature in the fact that billions of humans are responsible (though very unequally) for the misery of billions of other humans. The water of the Flood doesn't come from on high to drown people's sins; the sinful people themselves are the ones whose multiform actions come to drown the sinful people. The end time lies in ourselves, we who impose it on ourselves through a stupefying effect of blind reflexivity. Each one of us – in very different proportions depending on whether we are rich or poor, influential or impoverished, wasteful or ascetic – each of us is at once an innocent victim, an evildoing sinner, and an exterminating angel.

If it is indeed true that, in the evangelical texts, the theme of the end time totally modifies the customary course of morality, good sense, and politics, then I believe we can conclude that the same is true today. No matter what impression we may have of the contradictory predictions (I was going to say prophecies) about the ecological crises, one thing is certain: all questions of morality and spirituality find themselves once again subjected to a new eschatological constraint. It is impossible to define what is lasting and what is transitory, what is high and what is low, what is good and what is bad, what is human and what is inhuman, without subjecting it immediately to the formidable injunction: "Watch out! The time is near when you risk losing the Earth." In other words, the hour of truth is approaching for any spirituality oriented toward Heaven: if you are truly detached from any terrestrial condition, as you claim, what will remain of your soul? The great virtue of ecological and eschatological crises is that they finally submit dualism to this ultimate test, the veritable *experientia crucis*: the body is going to be taken away from you for good, and we shall finally see what you have left! Only the followers of the Solar Temple cult can rejoice at the announcement of such a translocation away from the conditions of existence of the blue planet. For all the others, if they lose the Earth – at least I find it hard not to suppose this – they will also lose their souls. Certain "humans" also see themselves as "sons of God," but they are all, in the end, "earthlings." If I dared, I would say that the imitation of Jesus Christ consists in acting "like him": that is, in turning finally toward the endangered Earth and abandoning the tranquility of Heaven.

But what does it mean to "turn toward the Earth"? Does it mean "turning toward nature," going "back to nature"?

Many ecologists, whether superficial or profound, accuse Christian theologies (but also Jewish thought) of being responsible for the modern *hubris*, since they are thought to have favored the development of science and technology (a paradoxical accusation for those who also accuse Christians of obscurantism . . .) while offering to humans' frenzied drive for domination a field of action that no counter-power could come in to restrain.

Without the theology that has put all creatures under the indisputably dominant sway of Adam alone, we would never have ravaged the planet to this extent, the critics say. The profound immorality of all Christian morality, they assert, comes first of all from this separation between enduring spiritual salvation on the one hand and the simple transitory material that serves only as its framework or décor. We would owe the sordid materialism responsible for all the catastrophes to the various Christianities, Catholics first and Protestants next. All Christians, in other words, would be James Watts, indifferent to the matter that they have learned to master and thus to scorn.

That is what authorizes those same critics to seek the solution of the ecological crises in a new naturalism; they imagine they are rediscovering the tendencies and sometimes the rituals of a dreamed-up paganism, which, rather mysteriously, would have managed, if we had not been chased away from them by the missionaries, to allow us to be "still living in harmony with nature." Only St. Francis of Assisi has found grace in the eyes of these critics. But don't worry, I won't say any more about St. Francis, about his wolf, his birds, his "sister the Moon," than I'll say (disparagingly) about Descartes' texts on "becoming the master and possessor of nature."

Without overlooking the mercantile foolishness of poor James Watt, we would have had to forget all religious history, and I'll add the history of the sciences, to avoid seeing that the entire cosmos has always been mobilized in the grand story of the Incarnation. Never just humans alone. If it is true that scholarly theology, thoroughly rationalized, at least in the Western tradition, has followed the movement of modernist philosophy and become more and more anthropocentric, the fact remains that all Holy Scripture, all the old religious art, remains "cosmocentric." In becoming Kantian, it is true, theology, and perhaps the spirituality that followed, has reversed the very meaning of the term "Copernican revolution" by turning all knowledge, morality, and aesthetics back to revolving around human categories alone. This doesn't mean, however, that in an infinitely deeper sense, and despite the Galileo affair, the real Copernican revolution had not been accomplished, this time in the right direction, and well before Copernicus, by those who had made the cosmos as a whole the center around which the great story of creation ought to turn in the first place. It is indeed this story that is "groaning with the pains of giving birth." Not only humanity. When the Holy Spirit is invoked, it is not so that it will come to wipe the tears from the faces of humans alone, but rather that "it will come to renew the face of the Earth."[4] The quarrel between science and religion scarcely hides another much deeper quarrel between those who speak above all of the cosmos (the sciences *and the religions*) and those who speak *only* of humans and their interests. Dare I say that the real quarrel is located from now on between the cosmocentrists (scientists and religionists alike) and the anthropocentrists (not to say the "humanists")? Since the humanists are without a cosmos, stuck like the members of the Solar Temple on the meeting with their comet, can we say that they even have a morality or a spirituality? Let me risk going even further: can we still say that a "humanist morality" exists, now that ecological eschatology has come knocking at the door?

The critical ecologists are quite wrong to complain that the Church has taught the rapacious capitalists "scorn for nature" instead of teaching them to respect it; it is, on the contrary, by making respect for natural law the only curb on human malfeasance that the Church has lost the world, which grants at best a polite assent to what she may say about morality – and takes none of it into account. And this is happening at the very moment when ecological eschatology is once again suspending all the old demands of morality and common sense and is finally making the wheel of all our worries turn around the cosmos once again. The appeal to nature, to natural law, often seems to serve as a touchstone for a whole other series of controversial questions, even as nature, when it is taken out of the hands of the scientists, never has the legal character of an unchallengeable decree. Sometimes one even has the impression that dogmatic views are more rationalist than the most rationalist of scientists: the task of defining not only truth and falsehood but also good and evil has been delegated to the laws of nature. Just as respect for nature, as I have shown elsewhere,[5] has lost the ecologists by leading them to embrace the chimera of their worst enemies, similarly the Church, by clinging to nature, risks losing its profound vocation, which is Creation "undergoing labor pains."

Returning to the Earth, as we can see, does not mean the same thing at all as "going back to nature," "respecting nature," "sticking with nature." The anthropologists have recently freed us from the cliché according to which there used to be happy populations that lived "in harmony with nature," just as the archaeologists have dispensed with another cliché holding that there once were pagans who "respected nature"; from Easter Island to the lakes of the Jura, their lesson is, alas, the same: always further advanced in destruction, down to the last tree, the last fish, the last wild hare. If we are to believe Philippe Descola's superb book,[6] nature, or rather naturalism, is a cultural exception limited to a segment of humanity, our own (and even then, only if we admit that we have been modern, which I contest), and it constitutes only one of four ways for a collective to maintain relations with nonhumans. If we prefer to understand nothing about ecological eschatology, if we prefer to remain blind three times over – scientifically, religiously, and politically – to the major event constituted by the ecological crises, one thing is clear: it suffices to think that we are dealing with nature, with its laws, its protection. The fact that there are appealing neo-pagans who seek to "go back to nature" by eating only wild wheat should not make us go backward any more than hearing members of the Curia seek to resolve the huge question of human reproduction by "natural methods" alone . . . With nature, that mixed bag of Roman law with nature parks, Cartesian dualisms, market calculations, green tourism, "organic" labels, there is decidedly nothing to be done. Let's leave that nature behind. What the present eschatology is bringing to an end, thank God, is "Nature": the end time has come, we are no longer dealing with nature – yes, "nature will pass away": it has already passed; everything that constitutes it has already been transfigured! The great god Pan is dead.

The dogma of the Incarnation has never meant, as far as I know, that God had been incarnated "in nature," but rather that he had relaunched the movement of his creation. Which is not at all the same thing. What differentiates creation from nature is not, as one might have thought at first glance, that creation is attributable to a God and nature to no one. The real difference, as the great philosopher Alfred North Whitehead saw clearly,[7] lies in the theory of action that serves as a model for understanding the relation between causes and effects. Many of those who assert that they "believe in a Creator God" and claim the right, for that reason, to look down on "scientists," "reductionists," and "mechanists," with their strict linking of causes and effects, which is "meaningless," they say, do not notice that they are almost always making their Creator God play exactly the same causal role as the one for which they are reproaching their adversaries. Their God creates nothing, he only "causes" effects, which are entirely determined and cannot in any way react to their causes. Conversely, there are many explanations said to be "scientific," as "agnostic" as one might wish, that offer an entirely different picture of the relation between causes and effects, by leaving to the effects, the happenings, the power to turn back on their causes – under various names such as process, emergence, retroaction – but for which the word "creation" is ultimately not so inappropriate: what counts, in all these processes, is that the creator is implicated in what is created, that the creator is not master of what is created, that the creator risks losing the creation and risks being lost along with it. Thus despite the American quarrel between creationists and evolutionists (what is the difference, moreover, between the upholders of a final cause and those who adhere to an antecedent cause, since they agree on what is essential: the mode of action of causes?), the big question is not what meaning must be added to or withdrawn from the cosmic adventure, but what meaning comes, in the course of creation, from what emerges in that creation and what has, precisely, no cause. In other words, one can be infinitely closer to creation as a Darwinian (in Darwin's sense, obviously, not in that of the neo-Darwinians) than by crushing all effects under a God that is the unique cause but by no means a creator. The great dogma of the Incarnation is infinitely better served, and infinitely more piously celebrated, by the process of a Creation freed from a causational God than by any recourse to the ancient mythology deployed in the stories in the book of Genesis. (Teilhard de Chardin would have excelled at this exercise, I am convinced, if he had not been trapped in the obligation to prove his orthodoxy with each of his metaphors.)

What has closed off this path to the renewal of the Faith is the fear of losing that exalted transcendence and of "slipping" or "falling" into pantheism: *Deus sive natura,* "God or nature." But that fear itself, a fear that has paralyzed all moral philosophy since the Kantian counter-revolution, stems solely from a quite false idea of creation conflated with nature. The notion of nature, in fact, does not paralyze just those religious believers who are obliged to counter it by placing the transcendence of their God outside of nature, that is, nowhere, but it first stifles the scientists, who can no longer do justice to the phenomena whose emergence they study everywhere. Virtually no one realizes in fact that the philosophical idea of matter we have been embracing for three centuries is as calamitous as our notion of mind, and that neither relates in any way, any longer, to what cosmology, physics, chemistry, biology, geology, geography, or the neurosciences are proposing today as interpretations of the cosmos. If the God of classical theology has trouble holding up in nature as it has been depicted from Locke onward, this is even more the case with the phenomena being discovered and revealed every day in scientific journals.[8] If it is true that nature crushes religion, then it stifles the sciences more forcefully still. And if ecological theology has a job to do, it is that of liberating not only religion but also science from the "weight of nature." What a waste: the construction of a whole theology, a whole apologetics, in order to distinguish "divine transcendence" clearly at last from "material immanence," when matter itself, or rather, matters, have undergone such transformations that they are still more distant from classic materialism than classic materialism is distant from the old causational God. (There is a lot more to say on the history of matter's conflation, in practice, with the modes of access that knowledge requires. I refer you to Whitehead, especially his *Concept of Nature,* and Isabelle Stengers' remarkable commentary on that book.)[9]

Here again, science and religion turn out to be on the same side, or rather they are both split in two in the same way. If you pray to the Holy Spirit to come to renew the face of the Earth, don't forget that the Spirit of the sciences has already done that . . .; it might well be time for the guardians of the Incarnation to notice. Before seeking to leave this world behind by way of the virtual rocket of the Solar Temple, it would not be a bad thing to recognize that "the world here below" in no way resembles the one that spirituality used to try, unsuccessfully of course, to "transcend" (Teilhard again). Transcendencies abound, here below, and it is here that everything happens. Yes, it's true, the great task of religion is thus indeed to "free itself from nature," but not at all in the sense that it should liberate itself from creation. To free itself from nature, on the contrary, it has to incarnate itself further and rejoin the flesh suffering labor pains.

What difference can that possibly make, you may ask, for moral theology? A huge difference, for once we are freed from nature, it finally becomes possible for us to attach ourselves to the great question of creation, and first to that of artifice and ingeniousness.

What makes most ecological predictions (prophecies) about the end times more or less detestable is that the predictors want to make us feel ashamed for having innovated, invented, upset "the equilibrium of the planet" (another myth from which scientific ecology nevertheless freed us long ago by retracing the constantly disequilibrated history of all the ecosystems and, even, ultimately, of the cosmos as a whole). If we listened to the "prophets of doom," we would have to feel guilty for our excesses, we would have to suspend our crazy innovations and feel our limits at last, before returning in this way to a healthy sobriety. After the injunction to "be fruitful and multiply," now they want to humiliate us with "degrowth": "Stop growing, shrink, erase the trace you're leaving on this Earth, shrink your footprint ..." Very few believers still observe the Lenten fast? Well, it's to long centuries of Lent that you are invited today. The fasting that asceticism could no longer get from us by moral injunction is now going to be imposed on us by a new "respect for the laws of nature." It is not surprising, under these conditions, that ecological eschatology elicits only terror and discouragement. Not only have we sinned in frightful proportions "against nature" (as if one could sin against an idea!), but beyond that, to make honorable amends we shall no longer have the right to use the formidable resource that we have developed over some ten centuries: the transformational power of the sciences, technologies, and economies. After renewing the face of the Earth we are supposed to withdraw in good order and all become invisible and frugal. Whereas we have four or five billion poor people . . .

It is at this point, it seems to me, that our great religious tradition needs to come to the aid of the ecological movements whose sermonizing can guide us only to the desert. For those who have been incarnated in the created world to the point of transforming it from top to bottom, a lesson very different from "stop growing and get smaller" is needed. Since there is no "nature" to protect, but there is a creation to continue, then we can go back to the dogma of the Incarnation and take from it the fundamental lesson that where there has been sin, there also is Redemption. Ecological eschatology is a discourse of the end times, but it is not an invocation of the Apocalypse. Just as Christians have had to learn, in pain, grief, and disappointment that the "Coming of the Kingdom" did not at all mean "the end of the world," but rather that they were going to have to inhabit this "vale of tears" in an *entirely different way*, that they would have to take responsibility for an empire and soon for an entire planet, similarly it seems to me that the guardians of the Incarnation ought to understand that what is at stake in ecology is quite simply the resumption of the movement of creation: it is going to be necessary to take responsibility for precisely what religious people scorn the most, not the vale of tears, not the empire, but the sciences, the technologies, the markets, the globe. It is because we have made all the details of our existence artificial, and *fortunately so*, that we have to continue to be still more artificial. In a way that I acknowledge is surprising, ecological spirituality has nothing to do with Heaven or with what is natural; rather, it has to do with what is artificial and fabricated, that is, *with what is created*.

But what sort of creator do we need? You all know the story of Frankenstein, but perhaps you have forgotten that the sin of the creator, Victor Frankenstein, is not at all – as is often claimed and as he himself said in a gesture of hypocritical self-accusation – the sin of succumbing to hubris and daring to build a living creature from scratch. That is why, as he says, he pursues the creature (who remains without any other name in Mary Shelley's novel)[10] with the goal of exterminating him so he will not reproduce and so will be unable to invade the Earth with his criminal offspring. No, that is the venial sin that he is willing to confess, the better to hide the real one, the mortal sin. Shelley's novel goes much further than that: Victor's real fault, the one he hides behind his frenzy of contrition and behind his hunt for the man – or rather for the monster – is that he has *abandoned* the creature after having made it. Horrified by what he has seen in his laboratory, Victor has *fled*, and it is the creature, obliged to learn how to get along alone in a hostile world, who then becomes evil, monstrous, criminal. How do we know this? The creature itself says so to Victor when it finally meets him again on the Sea of Ice: "I was born good, I became bad because of you": in other words, "Why, oh why, have you abandoned me?"

The connection Shelley makes with moral theology, right in the heart of the English industrial revolution, is explicit. Amusingly, there is another link, which I learned about recently, with the climate: it has been asserted that one of the events that lay behind Shelley's story was the explosion in 1815 of the Indonesian volcano Mount Tamboura, which so thoroughly blotted out the sky for a year that the friends brought together by Lord Byron couldn't go on the excursions in the Alps that they'd planned for the summer of 1816 ... and were obliged to settle for creating dark mystery stories, thereby inventing the *roman noir*.[11] The first lesson is well known to all fabricators, to all creators: if it is true that humans are made in God's image, neither humans nor gods control what they have fabricated. No creators have ever dominated or controlled their creations. Surprise, yes; command and control, never. Nothing is more false, in this sense, than the adage *verum factum*, Vico's principle according to which one can know the truth in what one makes.

But it is the second lesson that matters primarily to us at this point: the true sin is not that of creating but that of abandoning one's creation to its own devices, that of fleeing with horror from the unintended consequences of our projects, and pretending, as Victor does hypocritically at the end of the novel, that he is going to "go back home" to tend to his garden and abstain from inventing from then on. Reread *Frankenstein, or the Modern Prometheus*: God himself did not abandon his Creation and indeed sent it his "beloved Son," and you, the Earthlings, would abandon your multiple creations, and would beat a retreat while duplicitously confessing your guilt? God loved the world, and not you? (He perhaps had a choice; you did not, you have no other Earths . . .). The only morality that should be invented is that of a Victor *who would not have fled* when faced by the monsters that emerged from his hands. Creation can be taken up again, loved, redeemed; it cannot be interrupted. As strange as it sounds, we need to *love* the sciences, the technologies, the markets, in short, what is artificial in an Earth whose face we need to learn to reshape. Prometheus we are, Prometheus we must continue to be, but this time, "made in the image of God." "Promethean" action could also be a Christian virtue? This is in any case the lesson that I draw from Shelley's forward-looking novel, a veritable *roman d'anticipation*.

Moreover, can we imagine the Genesis story reread and corrected by Mary Shelley? After having shaped those vases of clay and iniquity, those earthborn characters Adam and Eve, as stitched-together as the Boris Karloff creature whom the creator God, frightened by what he had done, left behind in what must have looked less like an earthly paradise than a cluttered laboratory? And we poor incomplete creatures would have become wicked evil-doers because we had been abandoned? The original sin that we are accused of committing would not have been committed by us, at the origin of the world; it would have been the sin of the Creator, guilty of not having clearly assessed the tree of Good and Evil: like Victor, he would have confused the act of creation with the immediate result without recognizing that every creation begins badly and wins its virtues only gradually, in a long thread of meticulous, cautious experimentation that requires attentive care and that one can never interrupt without sinning against hope.

The earthly paradise was not in Victor's laboratory but lies before us, perhaps. Like the technological innovations that I have learned to study, Earthlings are born ill-formed, badly put together. Man is born bad. The flight of his creators corrupts him definitively.

If I have not yet tired you out too much with my paradoxes, to conclude I need to face the most difficult question: "If you lose the Earth, then what good will it do you to have saved your soul?" You know better than I that no religion, Christianity no more than any other, is guaranteed to situate rightly the distinction of which it is nevertheless the definitive Revelation. Here is still another paradox, since all is finished and yet it must all be taken up again. Every religion is always in great danger of impiety. The history of the Church, of dogma, of spirituality, is the history of continual slippage, continual apprenticeship, continual invention in order to identify, always in new contexts, a distinction that had been believed, wrongly, to have been found, definitively, in a different context. From the "Mosaic distinction," to borrow Jan Assmann's expression,[12] up to our own day, this story, frightfully battered, has never come to an end – crucially, it *must* not end, for we would go wrong for sure if we suspended its flow. The history of salvation is not the majestic unfolding of an incontestable cause, but on the contrary a hesitation, constantly repeated in fear and trembling, about how to understand the message. From this viewpoint, the Apocalypse, eschatology, morality, even dogma, are only transitory ways of situating the radical break, the juncture that we are always seeking to install, through ritual and discourse, here, then there, then again over there. Yes, it is the end time, but this does not tell us what *time* and what *end* are at stake. "On what grounds can this generation be calling for a sign?"

This is certainly the case for the difference between the body and the soul – a provisional vehicle for a distinction that needs to be quickly transported elsewhere for fear that it may wither and die. But it is surely also the case for the difference between the High and the Low, between Heaven and Earth. It is probably such worn-out metaphors that Scripture seeks to identify with the vigorous injunction: "If your right eye should cause you to sin, tear it out and throw it away" (Matthew 5:28). If a metaphor, however venerable it may be, no longer manages to take in, to capture, to serve as a repository for the distinction between truth and falsehood that you are seeking, then it must be torn out, subverted, crushed. That is what Charles Péguy sought to do in his vast enterprise of renovation so that the God on High could finally be returned to his place, that is, here Below. *Clio*, we must keep on rereading *Clio*.[13]

Thus, it is surely the case as well for the sempiternal distinction between the transitory and the durable, the impermanent and the permanent, the secular and the spiritual. Is there anything moral, religious, Christian left in that worn-out and much-abused trope? Conversely, don't you feel how amply one could renew the whole eschatology by paying close attention to the set of vibrant metaphors that speak of the Earth and its impermanence? I know quite well how trivial it may seem, on this point, to allude to the exceedingly practical theme of "sustainable development." And yet why could that not, by the very inversion it implies, take in a portion of the distinction that invocations of the soul, of Heaven, and of permanence no longer manage to capture?[14] The sustainable is no longer what one must go off and seek by leaving the world, but what must be made to last by renewed care, by attention to every instant, by infinite precautions applied to our "development" itself. The great distinction no longer operates between the Low and the High, between Earth and Heaven (if the distinction were still in place, one could simply slip away, flee, hide, vanish); it has now become a distinction between the *carefulness* and the *carelessness* with which we treat our own artifices. You may find that this is not enough to capture the great difference between Salvation and Perdition. Unless it were precisely the Earth that must not be lost, that must be saved by being rendered somewhat sustainable. Permanence is found only in impermanence. God is in time: is that not the dogma itself? The affirmation is so stupefying that access to it must be constantly rekindled: "If you lose the Earth, what good will it do you to have saved your soul?"

Have you noticed the strange paradox, this one more political, with which I shall conclude? People complain today about "the abandonment of revolutionary ideas." It appears that the public at large no longer has enough energy to imagine other ways of living, that there are no more utopias, and that even the youth of today, prematurely aged, are resigned to accepting, like their disenchanted elders, "the world as it is." The world as it is? Really? This is amusing, at the very moment when the eschatological themes are coming to strike that same public at large more forcefully than ever before. We ought to know: on the one side, we are told that "the end time is near"; on the other, that "there is no more revolutionary spirit." If there is nevertheless something revolutionary in the spirit of the ecological crises as they multiply before us, it is the obligation placed upon us to redraw from top to bottom the totality of our existences, the architecture of our cities, the design of our ways of life, even the list of beings with which we are going to have to cohabit. "Renew the face of the Earth": is this not perhaps a revolutionary program? And yet there is indeed a difference between the theme of Revolution and that of ecological eschatology; moreover, it seems to me to be the same difference as the one between the Apocalypse and the end of time. The old political Revolution was radical, on the whole: total, all-encompassing, and all at once. Ecological eschatology is radical too, but in detail, slowly, and it strikes in a multiplicity of fields, through the reformation of a multitude of actions among billions of people. I confess that I find this second version of the end of time infinitely more revolutionary, more materialist, more radical, and in the last analysis both more political and more pious than the first.

You will forgive me, I hope, for having found no other path than this meditation on the meaning that must be given from now on to love for the Earth. It is to a degenerate viceroy that Claudel lends this astonishing injunction: "the Church defends herself with the universe!"[15]

Notes

Foreword by Frédéric Louzeau

1 See especially Daniel Bogner, Michael Schüssler, and Christian Bauer, eds., *Gott, Gaïa und eine neue Gesellschaft: Theologie anders denken mit Bruno Latour* (Transcript Verlag 2021): https://library.oapen.org/handle/20.500.12657/51234. Independently of Latour's works and appeals, we can find reflections on the theological repercussions of the new cosmology and especially of the Gaia hypothesis in the works of Rosemary Radford Ruether, *Gaia and God: An Ecofeminist Theology of Earth Healing* (New York: Harper-Collins, 1994); Leonardo Boff, *Cry of the Earth, Cry of the Poor* (trans. Philip Berryman (Maryknoll, NY: Orbis Books, 1997); Thomas Berry, "The Gaia Theory: Its Religious Implications" (*ARC: The Journal of the Religious Studies Department, McGill University* 22 (1994): 7–19; Stephen B. Scharper, *Redeeming the Time: A Political Theology of the Environment* (New York: Continuum, 1997); Richard Bauckham,

Bible and Ecology: Rediscovering the Community of Creation (London: Darton, Longman, and Todd, 2009): https://library.oapen.org/handle/20.500.126 57/58954.

2 Translator's note: The word reprise, translated here as "mending," can also be read as "renewal," literally a "taking up again" and making new.

1 The Great Clamor: Conversation with Antonio Spadaro, SJ

1 http://www.bruno-latour.fr.

2 L'Obs, no. 2933 (January 14, 2021).

3 Pope Francis published the encyclical Laudato Si': On Care for Our Common Home on May 24, 2015. An English translation is available at https://www.vatican.va/content/francesco/en/encyclicals/documents/papa-francesco_20150524_enciclica-laudato-si.html.

4 Bruno Latour, Facing Gaia, trans. Catherine Porter (Cambridge: Polity [2015] 2017).

5 Translator's note: COP 21 is shorthand for the twenty-first session of the Conference of the Parties, which coincided with the eleventh session of the United Nations Climate Change Conference. Held in Paris from November 30 to December 12, 2015, the combined conference produced the international treaty on climate change known as the Paris Agreement.

6 See Bruno Latour and Peter Weibel, Critical Zones: The Science and Politics of Landing on Earth (Cambridge, MA: MIT Press, 2020).

7 On the opportunity offered by the cosmological revolution for the renewal of evangelical preaching,

see Anne-Sophie Breitwiller, Bruno Latour, and Frédéric Louzeau, "'Adam où es-tu?' Prêcher à l'époque de l'Anthropocène," *Esprit* (June 2021): 193–204.

8 After a seminar on the sources of ecological insensitivity led by Bruno Latour and Father Frédéric Louzeau (2017–2020) and an international colloquium, "Gaïa face à la théologie" [Gaia Facing Theology] (February 2020), in 2021 the Collège des Bernardins in Paris created a Research Chair titled *Laudato Si' – Pour une nouvelle exploration de la terre* (For a New Exploration of the Earth), initially filled by Professor Gregory Quenet, a historian of the environment, and Fathers Olric de Gélis and Frédéric Louzeau, theologians. The program and the resources of the Chair are accessible at https://www.collegedesbernardins.fr/recherche/cha ire-laudato-si-pour-une nouvelle-exploration-de-la-terre–2021–2023.

9 *Translator's note*: *Où atterrir? Comment s'orienter en politique* (Where to Land? How to Get One's Bearings in Politics) is the title of a short book Bruno Latour published in 2017 (in English as *Down to Earth: Politics in the New Climatic Regime*, trans. Catherine Porter (Cambridge: Polity, 2018). During the pandemic, Latour designed and led a series of theatrical exercises he called "Où atterrir?" that developed the metaphor of landing. See Bruno Latour, "Where to Land after the Pandemic: A Paper and Now a Platform," http://www.bruno-lato ur.fr/node/852; for more information in French, see https://medium.com/@paideiaconseil/o%C3%B9-at terrir-m%C3%A9thode–2adf1dbe47b4.

10 See "'Adam où es-tu?'" pp. 200–204.
11 Bruno Latour, *Où suis-je? Leçons du confinement à l'usage des terrestres* (Paris: La Découverte, 2021).
12 See Vítor Westhelle, *Eschatology and Space: The Lost Dimension in Theology Past and Present* (London: Palgrave, 2012).
13 Bruno Latour, *An Inquiry into Modes of Existence: An Anthropology of the Moderns,* trans. Catherine Porter (Cambridge, MA: Harvard University Press, 2013).
14 A short version of this interview was published on May 7, 2022, in *La Civilta Cattolica,* no. 4125, pp. 295–303. The French version is available at https//:www.laciviltacattolica.fr/la-grande-clameur -entretien-avec-bruno-latour/.

2 Ecological Mutation and Christian Cosmology

1 This lecture builds on a number of conversations that I have had with Frédéric Louzeau, Anne-Sophie Breitwiller, Émilie Hache, and Pierre-Louis Choquet. It was first published in English in *Creation – Transformation – Theology: International Congress of the European Society for Catholic Theology* (August 2021 – Osnabrück / Germany (Theology East–West, 30), edited by Margit Eckholt (Münster: LIT, 2022), pp. 85–94.
2 This expression is taken from Michel Serres, *The Natural Contract,* trans. Elizabeth MacArthur and William Paulson (Ann Arbor, MI: University of Michigan Press, 1995).
3 *Facing Gaia: Eight Lectures on the New Climatic Regime,* trans. Catherine Porter (Cambridge: Polity, 2017).

4 On this very specific mode of existence, and its own mode of truthfulness, see *An Inquiry into Modes of Existence: An Anthropology of the Moderns*, trans. Catherine Porter (Cambridge, MA: Harvard University Press, 2013).

5 Ivan Illich, *Ivan Illich in Conversation* (Toronto: House of Anansi Press, 1992).

6 A summary of this transformation can be found in Bruno Latour and Peter Weibel, *Critical Zones – The Science and Politics of Landing on Earth* (Cambridge, MA: MIT Press, 2020), and in the exhibition bearing the same title at the ZKM Karlsruhe until January 2022.

7 *Translator's note*: In translating the French term "terre/Terre" as "earth/Earth," we have followed the author's choice of capitalization, which varies depending on the immediate context.

8 Vítor Westhelle, *Eschatology and Space: The Lost Dimension in Theology Past and Present* (London: Palgrave, 2012). One quotation among others: "Paul Tillich, certainly one of the great theologians of the past century and highly sensitive to cultural issues and values, went so far as to claim that Christianity brought about the triumph of time over space. He identified paganism with the 'elevation of a special space to ultimate value and dignity.'" (p. 10).

9 The expression is even found in *Laudato Si'*.

10 Jan Assmann, *Le monothéisme et le langage de la violence* (Paris: Bayard, 2018).

3 On a Decisive Overturning of the Schema of the End Times

1 For a recent scientific synthesis, see Jan Zalasiewicz et al., *The Anthropocene as a Geological Unit* (Cambridge: Cambridge University Press, 2019), and for an excellent summary for a general audience see Nicola Davidson, "Human Activity Has Transformed the Earth – But Scientists Are Divided about Whether This is Really a Turning Point in Geographical History," *Guardian*, May 30, 2019.

2 Michel Serres, *The Natural Contract,* trans. Elizabeth MacArthur and William Paulson (Ann Arbor: University of Michigan Press, 1995).

3 Bruno Latour, *Facing Gaia: Eight Lectures on the New Climatic Regime,* trans. Catherine Porter (Cambridge: Polity, 2017).

4 Cf. Mark 8:36: "For what will it profit them to gain the whole world and forfeit their life?"

5 See Susan L. Brantley et al., "Designing a Network of Critical Zone Observatories to Explore the Living Skin of the Terrestrial Earth," *Earth Surface Dynamics* 5, no. 4 (2017): 841.

6 See Camille Riquier, *Philosophie de Péguy ou les mémoires d'un imbécile* (Paris: Presses Universitaires de France, 2017).

7 See Anna Lowenhaupt Tsing, *The Mushroom at the End of the World: The Possibility of Life in the Capitalist Ruins* (Princeton, NJ: Princeton University Press, 2015).

8 Jan Assmann, *The Price of Monotheism*, trans. Robert Savage (Stanford, CA: Stanford University Press, 2010).

9 Eric Voegelin, *The New Science of Politics* (Chicago, IL: University of Chicago Press, 1987).

10 See Bruno Latour, "On the Cult of the Factish Gods," translated by Catherine Porter with Heather MacLean, in *On the Modern Cult of the Factish Gods* (Durham, NC: Duke University Press, 2010), pp. 1–66, and Bruno Latour and Peter Weibel, eds., *Iconoclash* (Karlsruhe: ZKM, and London: MIT Press, 2002).

11 Émilie Hache, ed., *Reclaim: Recueil de textes écoféministes* (Paris: Cambourakis, 2016).

12 See Bruno Latour, *Rejoicing: Or the Torments of Religious Speech* (Cambridge: Polity, 2013) .

13 See Harald Welzer, *Climate Wars: Why People Will Be Killed in the Twenty-First Century*, trans. Patrick Camiller (Cambridge: Polity, 2012).

14 This text was published in the journal *Recherches de Science Religieuse* 107, no. 4 (October–December 2019): 601–615. A version of the essay was written for a talk at the Institut Catholique de Paris, Chaire du Bien Commun, on Friday, April 6, 2018, at the invitation of Father Frédéric Louzeau, whom I thank, along with the group of colleagues he has been bringing together since 2017 at the Collège des Bernardins to explore the connections between theology and ecology.

4 If You Lose the Earth, What Good Will It Do You to Have Saved Your Soul?

1 See Hélène and Jean Bastaire, *Pour une écologie chrétienne* (Paris: Le Cerf, 2004).

2 See Jurgen Moltmann, *Dieu dans la création: Traité écologique de la création*, Cogitatio Fidei, no. 46 (Paris: Le Cerf, 1988).

3 *Translator's note*: The English word "gospel" comes from the Latin *bona enuntiato*, "good news," used to translate the Latin *evangelium*, from the Greek *euangelion*, which is the root of *évangile*, the French word for "gospel." The word "apocalypse" is from the Greek *apokalupsis*, "uncovering" or "revelation."

4 See Jérôme Alexandre, *Je crois en la résurrection de la chair* (Paris: Parole et Silence, 2007).

5 Bruno Latour, *Politics of Nature: How to Bring the Sciences into Democracy*, trans. Catherine Porter (Cambridge, MA: Harvard University Press, 2004).

6 Philippe Descola, *Beyond Nature and Culture*, trans. Janet Lloyd (Chicago, IL: University of Chicago Press, 2013 [2005]).

7 Alfred North Whitehead, *Process and Reality: An Essay in Cosmology* (New York: Free Press, 1978 [1929]).

8 See "What is *Iconoclash*? or Is There a World Beyond the Image Wars?" in Peter Weibel and Bruno Latour, eds., *Iconoclash, Beyond the Image Wars in Science, Religion and Art* (Boston, MA: ZKM and MIT Press, 2002), pp. 14–37.

9 Alfred North Whitehead, *The Concept of Nature* (Ann Arbor: University of Michigan Press, 1957); Isabelle Stengers, *Thinking with Whitehead: A Free and Wild Creation of Concepts*, trans. Michael Chase (Cambridge, MA: Harvard University Press, 2011 [2002]).

10 Mary Wollstonecraft Shelley, *Frankenstein* (Project Gutenberg, 1891 [1818]).

11 See Henry Stommel and Elizabeth Stommel, *Volcano Weather: The Year Without a Summer* (New York: Simon and Schuster, 1983).

12 Jan Assmann, *Moïse l'égyptien: Un essai d'histoire de la mémoire* (Paris, Aubier, 2001).
13 Charles Péguy, *Clio* (Paris: Gallimard, 1931). See Bruno Latour, "Charles Péguy: Time, Space, and le Monde Moderne," *New Literary History* 26, no. 1 (2015): 41–62.
14 See Dieter T. Hessel and Rosemary Radford Ruether, eds., *Christianity and Ecology* (Cambridge, MA: Harvard University Press, 2000).
15 This text was originally published as "Si tu viens à perdre la terre, à quoi te sert d'avoir sauvé ton âme?" in Jacques-Noël Pérès, ed., *L'avenir de la Terre: Un défi pour les Églises* (Paris: Desclée de Brouwer, 2010), pp. 51–72. As the text was presented as the inaugural lecture at the colloquium "Eschatologie et Morale," held on March 13, 2008 at the Institut Catholique de Paris, I have maintained the oral style to some extent. I thank Jérôme Alexandre, Christophe Boureux, and Izabella Juraz for their advice, which my ignorance, alas, has sometimes kept me from following. The epigraph is from Paul Claudel, *The Satin Slipper,* trans. John O'Connor in collaboration with the author (New York: Sheed and Ward, 1945), Day 2, scene 5, p. 94.